FIXING THE

FUNNY BONE:

The G.R.I.T. Method to Heal with Humor

Jennifer J. Keith

Gremlyn Productions

For information about Gremlyn Productions and/or Jennifer J. Keith, please contact PO Box 312, Lincoln, Illinois 62656 or jenniferjkeith.com

Cover design by Iliyana from Wonderburg Creations
Manufactured in the United States of America

ISBN 979-8-9852725-7-4
ISBN 979-8-9852725-8-1
ISBN 979-8-9852725-9-8

DEDICATION

for Ryan, Gracelyn, and Emersyn

You were my dream before I knew how to dream,

and you still are.

FIXING THE

FUNNY BONE:

The G.R.I.T. Method to Heal with Humor

Jennifer J. Keith

TABLE OF CONTENTS

INTRODUCTION

Why can't life be like a romantic comedy?

After waiting until I was nearing 30 to find my forever boyfriend, I anticipated the proposal bliss that only soap operas and romantic comedies portray better: the gazebo overlooking the pond, the ring sparkling in what was left of the setting sun, scripted words that highlighted me (my favorite topic), and hearts swelling from anyone who heard the repeated tale no matter how many times it was repeated.

Instead, I was dating a pragmatic, practical, thoughtful, researcher, executor of well-thought-out-plans - someone who doesn't thrive on spontaneity, let alone LIKE surprises - he wanted to give me the ring IN THE JEWELRY STORE.

Here I am - the director of my own proposal, I GIVE him the proper script essentially, complete with settings and critical lighting cues - when to pick up the ring, where to take me at 5 p.m. to maximize the setting sun, the obvious answer of my acceptance. I let him choose his own words.

But as we arrive at the gazebo and begin to walk up the stairs to fiance'd bliss, we notice it is flanked with teens boys, dripping with a mix of marijuana and Axe body spray, bloodshot eyes, skateboards and half-devoured party-size bags of chips.

This is NOT in the script.

So I'm faced with a dilemma - climb the stairs to the gazebo and ignore the teens who have now discovered us as a new source of entertainment, or choose to give up my plans for an epic proposal and just go get proposed at the lakeside 50 yards away.

What do you choose?

What do you choose when life's plans don't work out as they are painstakingly scripted?

I remind myself that despite most of the script not going according to plan, I at least don't have to recast the leading man, for now, and stomp down to the lakeside, dejected, annoyed, with the sounds of cool ranch chips crunching in my wake.

A disappointed yet determined fiancé-to-be, I plop down on a beautiful bench, a calming ripple of water splashing ever-so-softly, the ring picking up the setting sun in all its shiny edges, words of love being expressed so beautifully, my beloved dropping to one knee and the unmistakable sound of his khakis ripping completely down the middle.

He is mortified.

I am overjoyed.

Not by the engagement ALONE, but truly because I now had a story - not the fluff-filled Hollywood version I wrote - even better - a FUNNY story, the one that rings true for me, for my husband (although he hates the story and denies it ever happened).

Don't worry - I have affidavits from the teens to verify.

Murphy's law is in full effect with a twist - anything that can go wrong can be funny - and funny is memorable.

* * *

The "funny bone" isn't really a bone at all.

It's a nerve in the elbow that if hit in just the right spot, you get a tingling or prickly sensation, almost a dull pain. It's temporary but painful – difficult to forget.

The ulnar nerve lets your brain know when it's bumped against the humerus bone, the long bone that runs from elbow to shoulder. We usually feel the impact in our 4th or 5th fingers as that's where the brain transmits the pain signal.

The nerve, on the other hand, travels much farther than just in your elbow. That nerve starts in the spine, runs up through the neck and down the elbow to the 4th and 5th fingers. The main objective of this nerve is to control the sensation in those fingers in addition to help the muscles in your hand control fine motor skills and grip.

So it's definitely an important part of our anatomy.

But, like anything else, when we hurt, it can last a while

We connect this "funny" sensation with a funny-named bone - the humerus - and the nickname of "funny bone" was born.

There really isn't anything funny about it though, not when we hit it and it instantly feels like ice cubes flowing through the veins and then an electric shock we assume only lightning can provide.

It hurts.

A lot.

But the good news is, it's temporary.

It's short term.

The pain goes away.

The memory may not, not for a long time, and it may dictate how we tenderly approach a situation again where the funny bone was bumped and caused us pain.

It teaches us.

Sometimes we get the message.

Sometimes we don't.

Over the years, I have hit the actual funny bone numerous times, and I have also discovered that humor can be a superpower to help you not only heal from the pain of loss and trauma but also to enhance the memories that linger and trigger.

Trauma is not funny.

Let's be very clear here.

BUT if we find pockets of joy, of laughter, of humorous situations around those dramatic, traumatic, painful moments, when we visit those memories, or process those memories, or experience a triggering event that calls those memories to the surface again, they may not seem as devastating as they once were.

The G.R.I.T. method, detailed in this book, is one I developed over years of struggle and laughter.

Dolly Parton's character Truvy in the 1989 film Steel Magnolias says, "Laughter through tears is my favorite emotion."

I wondered for years if I was the only one - the only one who laughed and cried at the same time, and not just laughing at inappropriate or "wrong" times or crying because I laughed so hard.

That movie convinced me that it was a normal thing to do, something even adults struggle with, and it sparked my interest in learning more about laughter as emotion and its role in processing grief and trauma.

So I gift to you the benefit of years of research and experiences that taught me the keys to processing grief and trauma with humor.

It's also permission for you to experience grief with EVERY type of loss.

It's okay.

You're okay.

Trauma
and
Loss

CHAPTER ONE

Loss is Sticky

The white, sticky puddle starts to bubble in the sun.

The little girl's tears splash below, creating a ripple in the puddle.

Her sobs make her mom wish they had enough money to buy a replacement treat.

But alas, they do not have it.

A kind passerby wants to help. Offers to buy a new cone, but the mom's pride is too great. A polite decline and the passerby moves along.

The mom bends down and tells the girl, "It's okay to cry. You lost something important."

And then she draws a frowny face in the sticky mess on the ground.

The mom knows this is just an ice cream cone, but to the girl, it's summer, it's freedom, it's a treat, it's delicious.

And the ground is now enjoying it.

Even if the girl and her mother are not.

The mom hugs the girl, dries the tears and promptly steps unintentionally into the mess.

She leaves sticky shoeprints on the hot concrete sidewalk for at least a block.

And that's an example of loss.

It can be an ice cream cone dropped to a sidewalk on a hot, sunny, July day,

It can be a family member no longer in your life.

It can be a dream that cannot come true.

It can be a life-changing diagnosis that alters all future plans.

It can be a job that turns toxic and no longer is fulfilling.

It can be a marriage that is not a partnership as promised.

It can be a relationship with a friend who moves away.

Loss and its feelings of despair and loneliness are universal. What is not universal is how we cope with those losses, because the severity of those losses and the personalities of those who suffer them are different each time.

We can process the losses in healthy ways, and just as easily, we can process them in unhealthy ways.

In this book you will be reminded of the steps we need to go through to process the losses and possibly turn them a little degree or two toward something lighter and more humorous.

A girl's ice cream cone disaster followed by sticky shoeprints or ripped pants after a successful proposal may lend themselves to help us find the funny faster and easier than other examples, but they both deserve their losses to be grieved.

Even if you don't remember when or where you first heard about the stages we go through to process loss or attribute it to the right psychologist, you know what must happen, what you must go through to get through the pain, to process it.

The girl who dropped her ice cream, and the girl in many other stories in this book, is me, but the child in your stories is you. Those children live inside us and carry with them the grief and sadness of those memories.

Our memories are connected to emotions, connected in our brains in the amygdala, inside the medial temporal lobe, just in front of the hippocampus. The amygdala plays a large part of regulating those emotions and anticipating the emotions based on previous experiences.

Most emotions have an energy, positive or negative, and an intensity, low to high, that triggers the brain's response. The prior knowledge of previous losses or our reactions help steer the brain to our next reaction.

The commonly discussed fight or flight response to fear or danger stems from prior knowledge - learned or experienced - and can even include freeze. Fight, flight or freeze are all defense mechanisms, feedback resulting in fear conditioning, value from experiencing or watching others' responses to scary situations, real or fictional.

When we react, imprints of our behaviors are formed on the amygdala, so that when a similar situation occurs, our brain has a template on how to respond.

Based on all that information, the emotions expressed can be similar as you experience a new trauma or loss, because your brain is learning from each new event, trying what it did previously to see if that works. The brain does not decipher all the details and nuances of a new loss or trauma, but rather uses what it learned from last time, from the imprints of the previous experiences, to provide an emotion for this new one.

Our brains have these imprints - and two imprints are the strongest. Those memories with trauma or those with humorous situations are not only the easiest to access but also the ones which have created the most imprints.

Those two types of memories stay with us longer than any other.

So, if we must remember the traumatic ones anyway, the G.R.I.T. method can empower us to be able to cushion them in a little bit of laughter or levity, surround them in a bit of softness, so they are not as painful when they are undoubtedly accessed again.

Our coping strategies with loss are as varied as we are.

In fact, there are also varied descriptions of grief and processes - from 4 steps to 5 stages to even 12 processes.

We will examine them all together and help you create a plan on how to process your grief, move through the grief, find connections with others, create new experiences and memories, and find the funny faster.

Here are the basics.

G.R.I.T. stands for Grieve, Relate, Invest and Transform, and it was developed by me for me and for you.

We are not promised trauma-free lives.

We have been through trauma. We have suffered loss.

We have grit, which is determination, resilience and perseverance.

We are worthy of the time and effort to work on this for you.

We deserve this.

We are entitled to have those memories accessed again to not be as painful.

We have earned it.

You have.

I promise.

This method will not erase your trauma or loss. It will not eliminate it from your life, your past, present or future.

But it can help you process the future traumas with a pain that can sting just a bit less than it did last time.

Your mental health improves when you process your losses, when you bring light into the darkness.

And this will walk you through those steps to help you help yourself.

You can laugh and still grieve. In fact, they are an important complement to one another. They both relieve stress and help you process what has happened to you and around you.

So give yourself permission to invest in yourself as you process the losses and move toward the funny.

It's also important to note what my G.R.I.T. method *won't* do.

It won't erase the pain.

It won't eliminate future pain, loss or trauma.

It won't disparage your experiences or make you feel guilty for moving through them.

It won't ask you to ignore, erase, eliminate or replace the memories.

It won't require you to find something funny in every situation. Many times, funny things do not happen or are not welcome during the trauma or loss. We find them later and add them to the situation, and sometimes we never find them.

Loss will ask you to consider all the emotions, all the feelings you felt then, and you feel now about those times, particularly anything funny, humorous or lighter than the deep, dark, painful feelings.

So, you know what we have to do first.

To get to the funny, we must start with the pain.

* * *

We never know when the trauma will come and find us, but we must always remember that it will.

Right after I graduated from college, I took a teaching job in a small northern Illinois town, population 2400. I was thrilled to be a teacher and be around high school students, who in most cases were no more than four years my junior.

In the five years I was at Amboy High, I taught English, directed plays and musicals, coached speech teams, and bonded with so many students, their parents, my colleagues, and community members. I particularly bonded with those who were also immigrants to the area. I formed a connection with Adelaide, a foreign exchange student from Bologna, Italy, and saved and scrimped to get a plane ticket to visit her during my spring break in 2001.

A few short weeks before, my ambition to follow my own dreams instead of only telling young adults to do it themselves drove me to make a massive shift in my career plans, and I submitted my resignation.

After five years, I was officially done teaching.

I loved the job, the students, the community, and what I did. I didn't want to leave those things, but I also started to listen to my own heart as it grew louder.

I felt a drive, a calling, to go to New York City and seek a 'bigger' life of being enthralled or immersed in theatre, the big city, and where film and television were made, in addition to Broadway.

I wanted to live in David Letterman's set.

I know that sounds stalker-ish, but I didn't really want to live in the Ed Sullivan Theatre on Broadway between 53rd and 54th streets in New York City. Knowing the exact address isn't exactly helping my defense.

I wanted to live in the bright lights of NYC that were represented on the set of CBS's Late Show with David Letterman for years. I was a faithful viewer – not a stalker.

I promised my mother at the beginning of making my plans a reality that I would find a job and somewhere safe to live. At the time of my resignation, I didn't know what those might have looked like, but I did believe I was making a promise I could keep.

As the oldest of three girls, I was already in college when my sisters entered high school, four and five years after me. By the time I was nearing the end of my teaching career, my sister Kristi was just beginning, starting in January 2001 as a high school English teacher herself in a small central Illinois parochial school.

Prior to my spring break trip to Italy, Kristi and I went shopping. She wanted to get her seniors a "you can do it" gift of Easter-type baskets of goodies. A graduation requirement at her school was for seniors to write a research paper, and they needed, in her opinion, a little encouragement.

During our excursion, we chatted about how her teaching career was just beginning while mine was ending.

I asked her what she thought about me going to New York City.

Kristi said, "I can't believe you're leaving those kids who love you so much."

She was right. I felt loved by those kids, their parents, my colleagues, the community, indeed.

I loved them all right back too.

Those five years were formidable years for me, ones that made me who I am decades later and a lifelong teacher.

Nevertheless, I also had other ambitions and goals and dreams, and I felt hypocritical encouraging my students to chase their dreams, when I had ones that had yet to be explored or even attempted.

I had to go.

The students knew that but didn't understand it.

Kristi knew that but didn't understand it.

I knew it but didn't completely understand it either.

That wasn't all I didn't understand.

Trauma was right around the corner, but I had no warning, no notice that this would be my last conversation with my sister.

CHAPTER TWO

Trauma Abroad and Abounds

I made my way to Italy, via Washington, D.C., via Chicago, which was still a three-hour drive from my apartment in Amboy, and a three-hour drive from my apartment in Amboy to my parent's house in central Illinois.

The distance is important.

While in Italy, I met up with Adelaide, her lovely family who welcomed me with open house and food and treated me so graciously from the start. I had never been overseas and to start with Italy was a dream come true.

I took tours around her beautiful city of Bologna, even going with her to her high school and being a guest speaker in her school's English classes one day. I had traveled with my theatre makeup kit because she had asked if I would speak to her school. As I worried about the language barrier (I knew some Spanish, but no Italian), I asked if there was anything that she would recommend I could show them. She knew my love of theatre and her school's limited theatre education and thought anything I could show them with makeup would be interactive, fun and accessible no matter what language I spoke.

She also told me that her peers were head-over-heels for the television series "ER," but no spoilers as they were a season behind in Italy. No Netflix in 2001.... if we only knew, we would have bought stock, right?

As it was one of my favorite shows, I had recently read an article where the 150th episode that had just aired in the states required an obscene amount of fake blood, extras and makeup injuries, and I thought that might be the best show and tell.

So I packed the makeup kit, with spirit gum, liquid latex, and red-colored corn syrup and was pleased with my plan.

I created black eyes, gave kids scars oozing with "blood," and showed behind-the-scenes techniques to the students for seven hours. They were enthralled, and I was thrilled I had maneuvered the language barrier for that small bit of time. I created the representations of trauma, all the while knowing they were fake. We laughed while making these memories, sometimes at my lack of Italian language skills, sometimes at the speed at which this native English speaker confused their Italian-born English teachers. I never dreamed that what I created in a high school day of fun learning would be my reality - the blood and scars and black eyes would be staring me in the face within days.

My first reward was to go to Venice to explore the next day, and then the following to get to Florence and see what Sandra Bullock always wanted to see in "While You Were Sleeping," my favorite romantic comedy.

I wouldn't get to Florence for at least 20 more years.

* * *

Venice was much smaller than I had expected, small pathways and a train to get you from city to city. It was overcast and lovely, and Adelaide and I walked almost every inch of it, returning to the train station minutes before departure.

Realizing I should probably use the bathroom before the journey back to Bologna, we headed for the toilets, and I realized quite quickly that Venician bathrooms are different than any other I had been to before.

You had to pay to pee. *A fee to pee.*

I had never found a pay-toilet in the United States before or since, and this was a first in my European travels. With the language challenge, I was completely confused and so grateful for Adelaide to be my translator and navigate me through the cue and pay my fee.

As I finished in a stall, I heard Adelaide's phone ring.

Cell phones were much different in 2001, flip in nature for the coolest of kids, and non-functioning outside of a basic paid network. My cheap-plan flip phone did not work in Italy. I had left it in Adelaide's house, but she had hers on for emergencies only.

This was an emergency.

And the call was for me.

She answered and handed me the phone, in the bathroom foyer with the attendants, just in front of the stalls of the pay toilets.

"Just wanted to let you know that Kristi was in a car accident," my stepdad said calmly, but I knew it had to be severe if he was tracking me down across the world.

"Okay. Should I come home?" I asked.

"It's up to you. She's broken her leg and her foot and she's in the ICU at Barnes Hospital in Saint Louis."

"What happened?"

"We don't know exactly. We are heading down there now."

My mom and stepdad had just discovered the accident had occurred, having tracked down the car before GPS was a thing, using his contacts within the state police network in the middle of the night. St. Louis was still a 3-hr drive from central Illinois.

"We will know more when we get there. Here's your mother."

Mom's reaction was drastically different, sobbing, hysterical.

"Kristi is dying," she choked out between sobs.

I told her I would be home as soon as I could, but I had to get back on the train to Bologna. We hung up, and my journey home began.

Prior to my Italian adventure, I moved every penny of my meager savings to my checking just in case I'd need access to it when I was overseas. Always the Girl Scout, no matter the age.

Internet travel arrangements were in their infancy in April of 2001, but I managed to book a new flight home for the next morning, with Adelaide's parents helplessly trying to assist and promising to take me to the airport in Milan within hours.

When I arrived at the airport, the desk attendant said I did not have a ticket after all. Adelaide arranged in Italian for me to change my existing flight for "bereavement" and got me the same ticket I thought I had already bought for a nominal fee.

Seventeen hours of travel through cars, planes, and airports ended at the St. Louis ICU.

Sunburned from an overcast Venice 24 hours prior, I joined my family for the next 30 days in the St. Louis Intensive Care Unit waiting room.

We became its hosts. At that time, there were no beds, or pull-out couches, or even overhead lights that could be adjusted for a family's comfort.

The trauma was overwhelming on horrible days, but as with any crisis that goes on, it became our new normal. So, we found joy in the simplest of routine things - rounds from doctors to give us updates, the shift changes, the maintenance and housekeeping employees doing their shift checks.

We slept curled up on loveseats with quickly bought and too-small blankets and pillows.

We comforted new members to the ICU community as they awaited news of their loved ones.

We avoided the "quiet room" to which a doctor summoned a family for updates that were rarely positive.

We became the unofficial and self-appointed greeters, hosts, and consolers while my 23-year-old sister lay in a coma.

For the next 30 days, my mother rarely left the ICU waiting area and never left the hospital.

We moved in.

We brought air mattresses and air pumps, blankets, pillows, food supplies in coolers, changes of clothes, toiletries, word search puzzles, and reading material.

We hosted family, friends, and strangers from all over the world.

We updated friends, bosses, and family members on her status, sharing more as we knew more. No social media to make it easier to alert the masses, but also receiving comfort, prayers and encouragement with every update.

We went back and forth to jobs, homes, and responsibilities, and would be called back at a moment's notice for the latest update, turn, or setback in her condition.

I taught those kids who loved me as much as I could, and comforted them.

We traveled to her seniors, the ones who loved *her* so much, gave them the Easter baskets she had purchased for them, and grieved with them.

We greeted her college friends who were finishing their semesters, our colleagues and loved ones who drove south to stay, comfort, and pray with and for us.

We cried, and we laughed.

"Laughter through tears," was our motto then, and still is.

Her friends told stories we had never heard of her mistakes and successes. All were enjoyable. Talking about her didn't sting then like it could have.

Yes, this horrible thing happened. Yes, we were living in an Intensive Care Unit's family waiting room.

Yes, we were waiting, and oftentimes had no answers except, "We have to wait and see."

When we tired of waiting and seeing, we dressed head to toe in "hazmat" suits and went into her room, protecting her against our germs, and visited with her.

We informed her of what had happened, what was happening, and what was going to happen.

We updated her on the status of her beloved St. Louis Cardinals.

We told her stories of things she had done that we loved, and we laughed.

We told her ways we missed her, and we cried.

We told her how much we loved her, and we grieved.

She never regained consciousness.

On day 30, it was our family's turn for the "quiet room."

There was no laughter in the quiet room, mostly silence.

We exited the room, packed our things, and loaded up the cars to go home.

It was time.

Her injuries were too severe.

She had lost too much blood in the initial surgery 30 days prior.

There was no brain activity.

She was gone.

* * *

There doesn't have to be laughter at the time of trauma - but I know you can, and I can, find it again.

As we processed the grief as a family, those related by blood and those related by friendship and love, we worked through the G.R.I.T. method, before it ever had a name.

We searched, sometimes unconsciously, for the joy, levity, laughter, light in the darkness as we lived it.

The pomp and circumstance of the funeral was up first.

The school where she has taught, her one and only post-degree position, canceled for all students on the day of her funeral, and almost all of the 250 students and faculty and staff came to the visitation and funeral.

We stood and greeted family and friends for hours, crying, hugging, and laughing with them.

My students came. My friends came. My bosses came.

At the standing-room only church during her service, the funeral director asked if we should order more fried chicken to feed the large crowd.

During the service.

We did.

We went from the church to the graveside.

My students, the ones who loved me so much, choked down sobs as they sang her favorite song, "Seasons (of Love)" from "Rent," at her grave. Acapella. As a gift to me, to my family, to everyone in attendance, to themselves.

And then very few came to the meal reception afterward, allowing the family to have their time alone.

We ate leftover chicken for a long time after.

We laughed just about every time we pulled out another portion to reheat. *Of course, we would be stuck with too many leftovers - the hosts with the most, always.*

Two of my students stayed after the burial to drive me the three hours home.

A high school senior refused to let me drive myself. He wanted to take care of me.

The other rode climbed in the back and buckled up. As the first backed out of the drive, he hit a tree branch that always hung a little too low, with the trunk of my car, denting it.

He didn't know it was there, I didn't think to mention it, and luckily not much damage was done to anywhere except the top of my trunk.

It would stay that way until and long after I had sold that car in another 18 months.

He felt awful.

I laughed.

This was something that could be fixed quickly.

My pain was not.

I chose to laugh because of the temporary loss of the smooth trunk back, and the absurdity of being upset at something so simply repaired.

Many theories of how we process loss and grieve it include bargaining - wanting to make a deal with those responsible, or assumed responsible, for the loss to reverse course, "correct" the wrongs.

It's natural to bargain, to blame, to think of how I could have punished or demanded restitution from someone else for this innocent action.

Through my G.R.I.T. method, at times when I didn't even know I was working through them, I found laughter reduced the stress, the anxiety, and their physical manifestations much faster than anything else I found.

While there are long-term effects of using laughter as a pain management tool, the short-term ones include the cooling down of the stress hormone cortisol and the release of endorphins in your body, making you feel easier the relief you get from a deep breathing exercise.

Even then in those difficult moments, I tried to remember other things than the pain - things that didn't replace or erase the pain but would cushion the pain. Over two decades later, it does.

It felt good to laugh, and it felt ridiculous.

But most things at that time did. And still do.

The survivor guilt. The processing of grief. The sorrow. The missing her. The "what if"s. The "if only"s.

They are all still there, no matter how much time passes.

My memories though sit now on a cloud of light and joy and peace in my brain's filing cabinet.

And that's why I'm still here.

CHAPTER THREE

Attack Your Dreams

While we sat in the ICU waiting room, hosting friends and family, we shared about a lot of things going on in our lives, and I informed many of my plans to leave teaching.

Most were shocked.

The follow-up questions were ones I had not prepared for and did not yet have those answers.

What are you going to do?

Where are you going to stay?

What are you thinking?

I knew of one location - New York City.

My high school theatre director stopped in one afternoon, and I informed him of my plans, my dreams.

He said, "I'll tell you what I told my son when he moved to Los Angeles to chase his acting dreams – 'make it or make peace with it.'"

Amboy High's administration hoped I would not follow through on my resignation, having held it from acceptance from the board of education since the moment I turned it in.

I asked them politely to accept it, thanking them for their love, support, and encouragement, but assuring them I would be leaving.

I packed up my apartment into my dented Ford Escort, and moved in with my parents, allowing me time to create my new plan, my new path, my new destiny.

In those days of internet communication being pretty much restricted to emails, I had exchanged a few with a college friend I had met in my English class who had grown daughters, one of whom was a nanny in New York City. She connected me with the daughter, who then reached out with her experiences, and I signed up at two nanny sites to find my safe living space to NYC through a built-in job.

Within two days, I had two serious emails and began correspondence with those families, ultimately agreeing to come out to NYC for a test visit to see if we both felt it was a good match.

I was treated extremely well and fell in love with the family, the atmosphere, and again with *my* city of New York.

I had only first seen her (forgive me for gendering a city, but she has the most famous statue in the world, who is also female) in person four years prior when I led my first of three trips with students, parents, faculty and friends to the East coast.

The first time I stood in Times Square in 1997, I knew I was home. I had to live there. It was David Letterman's fault.

As a fangirl of sarcastic wit comedians, I had hitched my wagon to David Letterman - studying him, repeating favorite monologues, creating my own top ten lists of parody and absurdity.

But what I wanted most of all was to live in his set.

Not realistically on the stage of the Ed Sullivan Theater at 1697 Broadway Street, because of the whole security thing, but in the land of make-believe, in Fred Rogers style, of being a part of the lights and energy of skyscrapers and neon and just big.

After meeting both families on the top two list of nanny possibilities, I agreed to a yearlong contract and moved to Manhasset, New York, from the city of Amboy, Illinois, population 2400.

Manhasset's population was nearly triple that of Amboy, but the proximity within a short Long Island Rail Road commute to my city where 8 million people claimed their residence was exactly what I wanted, what I needed.

It was August 2001.

Over the course of the next three weeks, I acclimated myself to the house I learned to call home, the twin 12-year-olds I was responsible for, and their community. After quickly creating a routine, getting the kids off to school and completing my daytime chores, I would oftentimes venture on the LIRR into the city.

Having pursued a journalism career early in my college life, I had found a love for photography and found myself wandering (with a bravado I didn't even know I had) into the International Center of Photography and signed up for classes. To be accepted, I was informed, I needed to meet with an advisor and show off a portfolio.

You know, the one I don't have.

I was told, though, I could purchase darkroom privileges prior to being officially enrolled and use it to prepare or augment my portfolio.

I did just that, and as a self-accountability measure, I gave myself until mid-September to complete said portfolio and, furthermore, created assignments for myself to complete in order to find the best images for the portfolio.

Once a teacher, always a teacher.

I'm shocked I didn't create my own rubric for grading.

Early in September, I took a double-decker bus tour of lower Manhattan on a sunny day. While the double-decker bus tour was my interest, I wasn't overly interested in touring the financial district as I had very little in the area of finances myself, but any of the other tours that day would put me too late for my return train ride back to Long Island.

I took numerous pictures of the southern tip of my city, my camera's shutter never slowing. I burned through countless, expensive rolls of film attempting to get the very best shots of all the architecture of the 100+ storied buildings.

It was September 6, 2001.

On September 7, 2001, I took a trip to the top of the Empire State Building, taking a different angle of lower Manhattan.

The weekend was spent traveling and exploring around Long Island, and Monday was resetting the kids and the house from the previous week, so I planned a trip into my city for Tuesday morning.

The weather was going to be gorgeous and great for taking images of the Empire State Building from the observation deck or even from The Windows On The World, especially early morning if possible.

Tuesday morning, September 11, 2001.

* * *

Monday, September 10, 2001 was spent taking care of the weekly preparations for the house - laundry, changing sheets for the kids, meal planning, grocery shopping, room straightening, and packing lunches for a Tuesday field trip. Their mom was heading overseas for a business trip, and their dad was working downtown in the city.

When the kids arrived home from school, it was snacks and homework and dinner preparation. After their dad returned home, I went and sat outside on the back patio and took a call from a former student, still in high school, who was still angry with me for leaving. We spoke for a while, as I reassured them that I had not chosen to leave those students, but rather to go to something.

I said, "I knew if I didn't leave now, I never would, and something says I need to be here. Now."

It was late when our call wrapped, as it was an hour later for me in the Eastern time zone than for them.

It took me a while to wind down my brain as I processed their hurt and abandonment. Normally, as I prepare myself for the next day, I set out my clothes and gear to make the morning a smoother transition - I am NOT a morning person, but a habit was formed early in life to have evening Jennifer help morning Jennifer by preparing the night before.

As I was overwhelmed with emotion and fatigue, I did not.

Tuesday morning was a scramble.

The kids had their field trip and were also not keen on getting up and moving in the morning. I dropped them off at school for their field trip, and drove directly to the train station, a very specific plan now in mind.

Take the LIRR to Penn Station, hop the subway downtown to World Trade Center, ascend the North Tower to Windows on the World, and take pictures of the Empire State Building from atop. My plan would put me in that vicinity around 9:03 am without any further delays.

I parked the car, quickly grabbed my things, and headed for the platform as the train slowed into position. I had to hustle to make it inside the open doors.

I made it, looked down at the bag slung over my shoulder, and immediately realized I did not have my camera bag.

No camera bag - no camera.

I hopped right back off the train as the doors began to close.

Furious with myself for not being prepared. Angry I hadn't set out the right bag last night so this morning was easier.

I marched back to the car and searched to see if I had the camera in the car and in my haste just didn't grab it for the train ride, but no camera.

I scolded myself. *How can you take pictures without a camera, Jennifer?*

I whipped the Suburban out of the parking lot and headed to the house on that Tuesday morning, a day I had intentionally avoided being at the house – their weekly housecleaning was scheduled on Tuesdays. Julia and I got along perfectly, but I thought it best to stay out of her way while she was working.

I parked in the drive, grabbed the wrong bag, and stomped inside.

Julia greeted me warmly, and gruffly I responded, "Hi. I'm not staying - I won't be in your way."

"You're not."

I entered my room, found the camera bag tossed in a corner, and checked its contents for all I needed.

I slung it over my shoulder and turned to leave.

It was 9:03 a.m.

The landline phone rang.

There was no answering machine at the house.

So I picked it up.

It was my mother, back in Illinois.

"Come home. Your city's on fire."

* * *

There was nothing funny about Tuesday, September 11, 2001, at the time, or even directly around that day.

The G.R.I.T. method doesn't require the actual traumatic event to ever be funny or joyful or painless.

Over 20 years later, the memories of 9-11 still sting for me.

But there is a bit less of the depth of the pain, sadness, and fear that were constant then.

As I was on the phone with my mom, Julia and I watched the television and the second plane take on the second tower.

"Madre de dios!" Julia shouted over and over.

Tears silently fell from my cheeks. The newscasters announced this was no accident.

I knew we were under attack, and I didn't know where to hide.

So we just watched the television.

For the first few hours, the phone rang and rang, people calling from all over to check on the family. The children's mother called in from the Czech Republic to let us know she was safely on the ground. The children's father called from midtown to say he was most likely staying in the city as it had been locked down. The school called to say the children had arrived at the field trip location and were promptly loaded back onto the bus and transported back to school and were safely there.

Former nannies, friends, colleagues, and others called to check on the welfare of the family, and I relayed information as quickly as I had it.

Then the phone went silent.

I would find out later that the landlines were overwhelmed with activity and were unable to handle the need and quit.

Julia found a television in another room to put on a Spanish-speaking channel to translate the news, but no matter the language, the site was the same devastation.

Families wouldn't greet their loved ones tonight as expected, and that was universal.

Julia went home to her family, and I went to retrieve the children from school. As I left, the father called and told me he had found a way out of the city and was coming home and would pick the children up himself. They needed to see him immediately, and he, they. I returned to the house and waited, watching the planes fly into the towers again and again, watching the towers fall again and again, until I couldn't do it any longer.

I went outside and sat on the patio chairs, where I had spent several evenings after dinner before. Then I heard very little - no planes overhead, no helicopters. Despite being in within miles of three major metropolitan airports, with grounded planes, I could *feel* the quiet.

I wasn't determined at that time, or any time soon, to move forward, to move on, to forget anything or everything that happened. I was still in the middle of the trauma, and at that point, I was there to survive and be grateful for the chances I had to do just that.

That's what we are supposed to do. To allow ourselves the time to grieve. There will be time when I can process and think about the laughter, with many traumas, I remind myself when times like these come up again, but first we must grieve.

That's the **G** of the G.R.I.T. method.

* * *

27

For nearly a month, the immediate area was quiet. The reduced flight patterns would last at least a month as security increased in and out of New York City.

The smoke was visible from the Port Washington area looking into Manhattan for weeks. On October 12, 2001, my sister came to visit from Illinois, and together we took one of the first tourist boat rides in lower Manhattan.

Combined with around 100 people, we toured the devastation firsthand from the safety of the boat, smelling burning fuel still 30 days later. It was silent from all of those onboard, and then spontaneously, a woman started singing "God Bless America," and several others joined in softly.

With my youngest sister by my side, and strangers watching the clean-up efforts at Ground Zero, I felt connected, assured, and comforted. Of course, I hated that others were suffering such tremendous losses, and yet, I was reminded I wasn't the only one who was going through such a time. I could relate to the pain others felt.

That's the **R** of the G.R.I.T. method.

It was then, even in the sheer darkness, that I, again, changed course. I signed up for courses at Nassau Community College in Long Island, taking drafting for technical production, beginning piano, and photography there as well. I started going into the city to seek new adventures, during the times the kids were in school, and after work and on weekends. I was able to view live theatre, first-run movies, and attend tapings of favorite shows, from "Live with Regis and Kelly" to "The Rosie O'Donnell Show" to "Late Night with David Letterman," finally, being in the room that sparked my interest so many years prior. I signed up to be a background actor for movies once the cameras started rolling again and worked three nights on the set of "Anger Management" with Woody Harrelson, Adam Sandler, and Marisa Tomei, at the original Yankee Stadium. Those experiences were things to look forward to, and were exciting, and new. I invested in myself and the things I had always wanted to do.

That's the I in the G.R.I.T. method.

As I moved through those stages, I began to find things fun and funny again, still not joking or finding humor in 9-11 itself.

I enjoyed the interactivity of a New York City movie theatre on opening night with a group of strangers. I realize that a movie is not intended to be an interactive experience always, especially one of the first premieres following the tragedy of 9-11.

In the sold out crowd, I took a seat with my popcorn for the debut of "Panic Room," starring Jodie Foster as Meg Altman, whose daughter is with her as they are being robbed in their posh NYC condo.

As Meg frantically races to her built-in panic room, members of the crowd started shouting to the screen.

"Girl, Jodie, get out the way" my seatmate screamed at the screen, clearly unaffected by two key facts: 1) Jodie was not even the character's name, and 2) Jodie (or Meg) could not hear any audience member.

I was completely amused and enthralled. And as it was a thriller, the comments continued until the final scene, when Jodie or Meg was successful in avoiding capture (apologize for the spoilers, but it's been 20 years, you should have watched it by now), and the wall-to-wall crowd celebrated with cheers and applause. I grinned ear to ear, having loved every minute of the additional entertainment the audience had provided.

Transforming those memories or at least finding the humor around those traumatic times is the T in the G.R.I.T. method.

Moments like these have altered how I feel and could have felt about living in New York City during 9-11. I processed them myself using the G.R.I.T. method - which is not a cure, but a way of reframing my thoughts and feelings about the trauma and loss in order to cushion the memory. Now when I access those memories, they are surrounded with moments of light and levity, rather than just the heaviness of the sorrow.

You can do it too.

We will walk through the steps together, and eventually, you won't need me to remind you of them anymore.

You'll be doing it subconsciously...without ever knowing it.

CHAPTER FOUR

Devastation Can't Last

Comedienne Carol Burnett credited her mother with saying "comedy is tragedy plus time." With enough distance, tragedies can seem or even be funny.

Think about a time when you have gotten potentially-inappropriately upset about an event or occurrence only to find out that, after some time passes, it was a non-issue. Something little or small, like the dent in the trunk top of my car on the day of my sister's funeral. Something easily repaired.

It may not have felt small at the time, but the space, the distance, the time between the feeling and the event have grown, and it now feels approachable by funny.

Some things definitely do not matter in time.

No, it doesn't matter that when I was growing up I could never find a keychain with my name on it - not because it wasn't a popular name, but because it was a popular name and was sold out.

Why did it seem like every parent named their daughter Jennifer or Angela or Michelle in the mid 1970s? There are other names, people!

I had at least two other Jennifers in every classroom I entered and with a difficult-to-pronounce maiden name that started with a P, I became Jennifer P. No girl wants to have a name that is or rhymes with a bodily function.

Surprisingly, that one still stings a bit, evidently, but I digress.

The consecutive months after the devastation of 9-11, living so close to Ground Zero, and trying desperately to not want to document the ordeal, were heart-wrenching. And healing, for me.

As I processed the loss and trauma of the year 2001 for my family, my city, and my world, I went through the stages of the

G.R.I.T. method, a four-step process to transform and heal from trauma and loss using lightness and humor to reframe, regroup or cushion painful memories, which gave me the perseverance and resilience to move through the trauma and loss, and then approach new trauma and loss differently when they arrived again.

When we encounter trauma or loss, we can use the four steps to transform or cushion our memories with humor and laughter and moments of light and joy.

First, we must grieve.

It is definitely tempting to skip over the grieving part, to just keep moving, keep working, business as usual, and in some cases, it is absolutely necessary.

But we must grieve - we must go through it, all its messy, hard steps and processes.

Then we must relate. Relating is about ourselves - finding something, someone, some experience that feels like what we went through or are going through. It doesn't have to be another person - it doesn't even have to be the same experience.

But it must be relatable to our experience or our processing of that experience enough to feel similar.

Then we must invest. We must invest in something new - without seeking to replace the event, person, item, or experience that was lost.

That something new can be any size, big or small, tangible or not, but something that pulls our focus and creates an excitement within you about the new, shiny whatever.

Then we can transform the trauma, or cushion it. Some traumas or losses cannot be and should not be transformed or reframed, but they can be near fun, light, or laughter.

The cushion that can provide when the memory of trauma or loss is accessed, and re-accessed, can help the accessor from feeling as severely.

Humor in many forms can help bring light to the trauma and losses we face. But we do have to train ourselves to know how to find the funny, and eventually, with practice, we will find the funny faster.

Psychologist Angela Duckworth, in her New York Times bestseller Grit: The Power of Passion and Perseverance, reveals her study of grit and self-control in order to predict achievement and success (2022). While she studied grit as a scientist to prove that the grit you are born with matters as much if not more than talent in a challenging situation, she believes you can train yourself to be grittier.

I believe you can train your sense of humor to find the funny faster, and not to replace the loss or trauma you feel, but as a way to cope with the gravity of the trauma or loss that you feel and package it in your memory as something more tolerable than it was at the time.

Going through the four steps of G.R.I.T. can train your brain to not only provide distance and light to previous trauma and loss, but create space in your mindset that allows you to encounter new trauma and loss with a different perspective.

* * *

While I wish we would never have trauma or loss again in the future, we know that it is inevitable, so preparing for it is best.

When I was in the fourth grade, I had a crush on the "boy next door." He was tall (for fourth grade), sandy brown hair, and a crooked smile. Athletic, smart, and, best of all, he was kind.

On a particularly busy morning, my mom was driving the car pool, which meant we had to leave even earlier than normal.

Let me make this very clear. I am not, nor will I ever be, a morning person. I don't understand it, and I don't want it in my life.

That particular morning, as I heard my mother honk the station wagon horn from the driveway, I knew I had to move very quickly or get left behind.

My mom ran an in-home daycare for the first 10 years of my life, and she was not letting her own child get in the way of her duties of taking other people's kids to school.

In a panic, I ran to the open living room, shoved my feet into two shoes I located from underneath the dining room, tied them, interrupted by a second blast of the station wagon horn, grabbed my backpack, descended the stairs, and climbed over the seats to the back of the station wagon, just in time - the car was already in reverse. No moment too soon.

We picked up the remaining four kids and pulled up to the parking lot for drop off. We had to cross a playground on blacktop to get to the school, and the warning bell rang as we speedwalked toward the office doors.

I heard the station wagon pull away behind me, but as I saw Sean in the distance ahead of me, I was focused on getting his attention.

Oh, that would not be a problem.

As he approached the door, he turned toward the parking lot, saw more students were coming, and held the door open for them.

Remember - I saw he was kind.

As I came through the doorway, he smiled and said, "Nice shoes."

I blushed.

"Thank you," I said with a giggle.

And then I looked down. I did have nice shoes, indeed, but they were not a matched pair.

On my left foot, I had a white canvas tennis shoe, tied beautifully in a bow.

On my right foot, I had a brown suede penny loafer, also tied beautifully in a bow.

My cheeks instantly flared red hot as tears welled up in my eyes.

I was going to cry in front of Sean, and there was nothing I could do to stop it.

Instead of heading toward my classroom, I turned left and marched directly into the office.

First things in the morning are not usually the best time to approach a school office with the hopes of compassion and comfort.

I had hope, but I didn't get compassion or comfort.

While the secretary allowed me to call home, my mom had just left, and I knew no one was at home. The age before cell phones was devastating for this reason alone.

Knowing it would be at least 15 minutes before I would even be able to reach my mother by phone, the secretary insisted I go on to class, assuring me she would call my mother herself and tell her the situation.

Embarrassed, with my head hanging low, I stomped upstairs toward the fourth grade classroom, tears still streaming down my face.

The office had alerted my teacher, and she met me in the hall, telling me to go wash my face in the girls' restroom, taking my bookbag gingerly from my shoulder.

"We can't change your shoes just yet, but we can change our attitudes," she whispered.

I tossed some cool water on my face, and then looked into the mirror above the sink, slowly raising my head to meet my own eyes in the reflection.

I sighed.

At the time, this was the single-most embarrassing moment of my life. *Ah, young Jennifer, there is so much more to come*, I would tell her today, but in that restroom mirror, this was it.

I mustered up the courage and walked across the hall back to the classroom. As I entered the room, I realized that the teacher had already begun the day's lesson and students were working in groups around the room.

I was eternally grateful. As I look back now, I realize that she had most likely orchestrated that moment to reduce my embarrassment. Teachers are rockstars.

I found my group, and no one was the wiser of my predicament, until the intercom buzzed around 20 minutes later, telling me to go to the office. My teacher could only do so much - she can't control the intercom system.

As was, and may still be, the tradition when a student gets called to the office, it's been a while since I was 9, the classmates fixed their eyes in my direction, some even oohing and aahing, wondering what I must have done to warrant an office visit so early in the morning.

Then they noticed the shoes.

And one pointed. And one laughed. I exited the room with lightning speed.

I descended the stairs and entered the office.

"Your mom didn't know which one you'd want, so she brought both."

The secretary handed me both of my matching shoes, a right foot white canvas tennis shoe, tied beautifully in a bow, and a left foot brown suede penny loafer, also tied beautifully in a bow.

Inside each one was a Pez dispenser. Wonder Woman.

Yes, indeed, my mother was a Wonder Woman.

Wonder Woman had been one of my favorite television shows in the late 1970s and early 1980s and merchandise was not easily found. My mom must have come across them at some point and stashed them away.

As Wonder Woman said, "so long as life remains, there is always hope....and so long as there is hope, there can be victory!"

The empowerment that my mother gave me, and the laugh that ensued, was all I needed to keep the original shoes on and go back to class, this time with my head held up, facing myself and my classmates head on. Rather than fear the laughter because it was directed "at" me and the situation, I embraced it and controlled it, directing it at "the situation" and the absurdity of picking the wrong shoes ruining my day.

The gravity of that situation is not larger than many others I would face in the next 30 years, but it taught me to approach humor in many different ways.

Humor doesn't have to make fun of us or ourselves to cause pain - rather, it can be used to play with the gravity or the severity of the trauma, loss, or gruesome reality, even if our tragedy is smaller or larger than someone else's.

The best part about humor is that we decide what works best for us.

Humor is universal.

The types of situations or stories or jokes that make us laugh or ease our pain may not be universal to everyone, but once we find the "right" type of humor for us, we can see how humor works for everyone.

Humor is healing.

The act of anticipating humor can reduce our stress up to 39%. That means, when someone who has proven to be funny in the past begins to tell you a story and you just know it's going to be good, your anxiety is already reduced.

Humor has the ability to connect us. The top seven characteristics we look for in an ideal partner, be it romantic or professional or anywhere in between, includes a matching sense of humor. We connect with others who share our sense of humor or surprise us, as humor is a surprise - what makes us laugh is when we cannot anticipate what will be shared or when.

When we connect with others, we have a stronger circle of influence with and over them.

Humor is power.

Morning Jennifer is not fun. Morning Jennifer is whiny, confused, sad, tired, and cranky. Morning Jennifer needs things done for her. Nighttime Jennifer to the rescue.

Nighttime Jennifer leaves the clothes that Morning Jennifer will wear on a hanger, so they are ready for the morning. Nighttime Jennifer leaves all the items that Morning Jennifer will leave for work the next day in a neat pile by her keys and purse.

Nighttime Jennifer straightens up the dishes and starts the dishwasher, packs lunches and places them in the refrigerator, and checks the schedules, double checking that her Nighttime Daughters have done the same for her Morning Daughters.

This was not always the way.

Prior to the "two-shoes incident," Nighttime Jennifer didn't exist. But Morning Jennifer paid a hefty price for Morning Jennifer's mistakes and Nighttime Jennifer was born.

Nighttime Jennifer was created to avoid embarrassment for the sake of not being prepared. Look, it's going to happen. Jennifer (day or night) is going to be embarrassed, but the least she can do for herself is to make sure "not being prepared" isn't the reason.

And I've been like that since that day in 3rd grade.

Since then, I have laid my clothes out the night before and I have done that for my children. In fact, every Sunday night, my children prepare their clothes plans for the week, checking the weather forecast and their schedules prior to making their plans.

We were not going to have arguments about what to wear every morning, and while they have freedom to select their own items, they are making those decisions when they are not in the "tired, cranky monster" stage we sometimes encounter in the mornings.

How else do I transform "morning monsters"?

Weird Al Yankovic.

I take popular songs that a "mom" shouldn't even know, as if, and I change the lyrics annoyingly and ridiculously, and make them specific to my children as I wake them or get them moving in the morning.

I should not be singing, and many people have asked me to stop. But I continue relentlessly, and I hope my children smile at least a little bit every morning when I do my off-key renditions of whatever new Taylor Swift or Cardi B hit strikes my fancy.

It's really hard to be upset when your mom is insane first thing in the morning, I rationalize.

I have used humor to motivate, to discipline myself and others, and to take something that could be uncomfortable and difficult and make it something that is a little slightly less.

Humor is a superpower.

CHAPTER FIVE

Humor is a Comfort

My mother's favorite phrase was "We may not have a lot of money, but we will laugh a lot." And laugh, we did.

She believed in humor as comforter, humor as entertainer, humor as disciplinarian, humor as life.

In our darkest moments, we found small nuggets of silly, of pain relief.

In one of the days hosting the ICU waiting room, my sister Julie and I were going stir crazy and running out of clean clothes - a great coincidence, so we opted to find a laundromat and spend at least an hour or two doing something for the family while also seeing different walls than the ICU waiting room ones for a bit.

On the way to the closest laundromat, we realized we also hadn't eaten anything for days that didn't come from the hospital cafeteria. A joy to be had was now fast food. Was this real life?

We came across a Kentucky Fried Chicken, and instantly, our mouths began to salivate at the thought that anything with more than two spices, like the Colonel's secret blend of 11 herbs and spices, sounded like heaven.

We calculated a large order with the thinking we could bring some back to mom and dad at the hospital, but also likely we would have time at the laundromat to down it all.

We pulled up to the speaker to place our drive-thru order.

"Welcome to KFC," said the teenage voice on the other end. "Just so you know, we are out of chicken."

Blink.

"What?"

"Yeah, we're out of chicken."

"Isn't that what you do?" my sister asked.

"Do you have anything else 'Kentucky Fried,' then?" I asked.

Then we burst into cackles and drove away.

Nothing to see here, folks. Just finding funny in the absurdity of a chicken-fast-food-chain-without-chicken in the midst of going through agonizing pain and trauma.

* * *

When I was blessed to have my own children, my mother's voice would echo in my mind as I worked with them, even if she was just across town.

Her love of trying to make things light or fun or lightening the mood in even a dark time was evident, save several moments in the ICU waiting room.

We hosted things - even ICU waiting rooms. We fed people - with actual food, company, and laughter.

The first time Kristi brought friends home from college with her, she brought at least five. She explained that she had told tales of comfort, laundry services, and home cooking, finishing the pitch with, "Follow me to food," and they willfully hopped in the car for the 2-hr drive "home."

First-time parenting is stressful, though. Trying to find the right food, the right comfort, the perfect things to do, say, feel. It's a lot of pressure. Even before social media, people shared their opinions on your parenting; social media just made it easier to be instantaneous.

So many things with parenting that are so serious - I mean, the life of a child is at risk. I loved being pregnant because everything that little baby needed, I felt I could provide and keep safe. Once they left my body, I couldn't say that anymore, and I felt that gravity.

When I think back to my mother's parenting, even looking at something like a spilled ice cream cone on the floor, when I thought it was extreme and disappointing and the end of something huge, my

41

mother allowed me to grieve, to recognize that I had lost something, something important to me.

I learned early on that grief and humor or fun do not have to live in separate planes, but rather can co-exist.

We are allowed, and should be encouraged, to grieve even the "little" losses, because they are all losses that deserve their place in the spotlight and to be processed.

If we ignore them, even the "small" ones, which are truly only small when we compare, which is also a nasty habit we need to break, they grow, or build, or add up and several small ones can combust when piled up together.

Distraction is usually taught as a coping or parenting technique for disappointment. It's what I read over and over again for when a baby/toddler was upset - distract them with something else. It honestly makes sense, because it moves us forward or away from the loss, grief, disappointment.

But many of us did not learn that as we age, we need to make sure that while we distract ourselves, we do not ignore or replace the loss immediately as a way to cope. We do not always just get a new ice cream cone.

As a parent, though, I want to teach my children, and other people's children, that they can come to me and share what is bothering them, that they will not be redirected or distracted with something else, something new, always. They can come to me for comfort, and I want them to seek that healthy comfort from me or others as a way to process that grief always.

Even a skinned knee or a torn fingernail or a torn piece of paper can be a really, really big overwhelming situation for us, especially for a toddler.

As a parent, I started a tradition - small injuries that were upsetting would be allowed their grieving time, the proper-sized and cartoon-decorated bandage, and the special scissors - my fingers used to "cut off" whatever body part was ailing.

We can wipe the tears or at least move through them a little faster with humor.

My strategy was not to argue or to fight, allow the feelings to be felt, but also lighten the mood.

The child knows when my special scissors come out, the ouchy must be ok, and that I'm not really going to "cut off" whatever body part is injured. It does make it a little more tolerable to laugh at the time of this loss, almost immediately.

Grieve

CHAPTER SIX

Sorry for your Loss

"I'm so sorry for your loss."

"I can't believe it."

"Call if you need anything."

"It doesn't seem real."

"Have you eaten?"

"You are in my thoughts and prayers."

When you're in the midst of sorrow and despair about whatever loss you're dealing with, friends, family, and strangers will offer words of comfort.

In my experience, words aren't all that comforting, but the idea that people care enough to try to help ease the sorrow by using words is extremely comforting.

Those words and the actions of those who care for us do not erase the requirement to go through the grief, however. And that's step one of our four steps to transforming your trauma.

Grieve.

Sounds easy enough. A one-syllable word, in fact. Small but very mighty.

Grieving doesn't look the same to all people or to all situations.

In fact, grief doesn't look the same to the same person and a similar situation - we evolve, change, and grow based on our experiences, so we will never be at the same point in our lives again with the same knowledge and the same level of expertise.

Grief helps us process the trauma and loss, no matter the gravity of the loss.

We grieve when our best friend at work takes another job. We grieve when a marriage ends. We grieve when something we hoped for doesn't materialize. We grieve when we lose a job, money, relationships, and people, whether temporarily or permanently.

No matter the size of the loss, we must grieve it to keep moving.

What does grief look like?

Elisabeth Kubler-Ross, in her 1969 book "On Death and Dying" said there are five stages of grief: denial, anger, bargaining, depression, and acceptance.

Denial is the feeling of being almost numb, very common in the early stages of a loss. Some people continue as if nothing has changed. Sometimes there are those phantom moments where it seems that the person is still around or the reality of the situation hasn't been felt yet.

Anger is a very natural reaction as well, as we move from numbness into feeling. We can be angry at the person or people we feel responsible for the loss or the ones who have left. We can be angry at ourselves for actions we *could have* taken but didn't or took but *shouldn't* have.

Bargaining is the process of trying to make a deal. Maybe, we think to ourselves, if I do this or that, they will change their minds. Maybe if I do this or that, or if I had done this or that, I wouldn't be going through this. The 'what if's that the bargaining stage causes us to recycle keeps grievers in this stage for a long time. And to no satisfying end.

Depression is the sadness and longing for what we no longer have. This is most commonly the "look" of grief. It can last a long time, days, weeks, months, years. It can come and go and come back again. Life can feel meaningless, and that can be powerful to overcome.

Acceptance is Kubler-Ross' last stage and is less the process of "getting over" death but rather the knowing we can live without whatever loss we have suffered, although also recognizing that that loss will leave us irrevocably altered forever. The acceptance is not forgiveness or forgetness. It is when some of the pain eases enough to continue moving despite what has happened, and learn from what has happened, many times where we make a pact to not let that sort of thing ever happen again.

Think five is too many stages? How about four phases?

In 1998, British psychiatrists John Bowlby and Colin Murray Parkes proposed the Four Phases of Grief: shock and numbness, yearning and searching, disorganization and despair, and reorganization and recovery.

Shock and numbness are the immediate aftermath of loss, where the person goes into shock to withdraw from reality and becomes numb and shuts down.

Yearning and searching is a phase with a variety of feelings - sadness, anger, anxiety, and confusion. The yearning for what has been lost is also a drive for the griever to fill the void created by the loss, sometimes in unhealthy ways.

Disorganization and despair are the first part of actually accepting that the loss is real. This phase can also send grievers into a withdrawal phase where they no longer participate in things they previously enjoyed, as a way to cope and protect their hearts from further pain.

Reorganization and recovery is when the griever determines a "new normal," not to eliminate the sadness, anger and despair, but notes its slow decline in intensity. The positive memories prior to the loss increase and the searching for meaning and answering "what if"s lessens.

What those scholars shared in common was that grief is not a linear process. While some of the phases or stages can last for weeks or months, some take mere moments and then are revisited as we move in and out of the phases and stages. Both phases and stages allow for the grievers to take as much time as needed to move in and out of phases and to take care of themselves in the processing of the losses.

Another viewpoint involves 12 emotions as we go through the personal transition through change, a curve researched and developed by chartered psychologist John M. Fisher (2000). In Fisher's transition, he notes 12 different emotional phases during a personal transition. While he doesn't specifically state that loss or bereavement is the cause of the personal journey to change, we know it has to be - and that loss doesn't have to be a death of someone close to be considered loss.

Fisher's model is also non-linear, showing that people often move in and out of emotions as they process the need for and the system of change.

Before the change occurs, or needs to occur, there may be *complacency*, where the connection to the person or the idea is dormant. This is usually evident when others react to someone grieving a loss in a surprising manner. For example, the person who didn't even have one conversation with a decedent but wallows and causes a scene at the funeral for the deceased, where people start to question, "Aunt Margie didn't even know Sue. Why is she acting like she's burying her best friend?"

What may look like complacency to others may be fear, worry, anxiety, busyness, and many other factors that have altered the relationship between the griever and the object to be grieved. Additionally, we may have just been in a state of complacency, expecting that the loss we have yet to experience will never happen, and then, as we have been warned, we don't really know what we have lost until it's gone.

From complacency, we move through *anxiety* where we question our own coping abilities. The anxiety part is where we realize that things beyond our control happened, and we cannot reliably predict the future. We thought we could, but now we know we cannot, and it's disappointing and unsettling.

Despite my growing up watching and adoring soap operas, I never really thought I'd be spending so much time in a hospital next to my sister, holding her hand, and watching her die. My complacency was in the thinking that those things happened to "other people" or in alternative realities that were very far away. The anxiety for me was when I realized that they do indeed happen to "my people."

We then must find the rationalization that we do have the capacity to move through whatever "this" is and find some hope to be able to continue. Fisher calls this stage *happiness*, where there is hope that something can change - even if it's scary. The happiness comes through strongly when we realize we are not alone in our grief or in wanting something to change.

When I realized after 9-11 that I was not the only one grieving the loss, there was hope that the strength in numbers would involve change and I wasn't in this grief by myself.

Humans require change and growth, even if it's uncomfortable. We remember the literal growing pains of our bodies as we move from infancy to adulthood, but we tend to forget them as time moves forward. That can happen with emotional growing pains as well, but we have to work through those. The beliefs that whatever was going on in our lives before this event that triggered such a sense of loss that something needed to change are now founded to be correct, and we have a slight bit of happiness in being right, but that is compounded by the fact that we didn't choose what the change was exactly, which is upsetting and potentially even more wrong. The happiness stage may be brief depending on the gravity of the loss being processed, but the change is going to happen regardless, so we find a hint of acceptance and hope in this stage. It, again, is not linear, so we may not experience happiness until much later in the processing of the loss. There is no right order to Fisher's change model.

Fear creeps in right alongside the happiness, because not only are you dealing with the loss or change, but so are other people, and no matter what we have told ourselves over the years, we cannot control them or their emotions. And that is frustrating. People will be acting differently, and you will be acting differently. What will that look like? What will that mean for you? When you finally thought you had figured it all out, and you were able to manage other people and their feelings, here comes this upsetting event that changes everything. Now what? Sometimes it will not look like something new, but it truly is as we have not encountered something like this before, and this needs to be handled. That is scary.

As we continue to process this change, we will view it as a threat. This event has the potential to change everything that we have worked so hard for and will continue to alter all the future plans we have made. It is a totally new, unexpected situation, and that creates a lot of questions about our future and where we are going now. We find that the "old" rules no longer are in effect, and we have to create new rules to deal with this new situation. That is threatening and unsettling as well.

Should we toss out all the strides forward we have made and revert back into a safe space or do we venture forward? Both are viable options - and there are positives and negatives to each. Choosing one doesn't solve all the problems, however.

All of these emotions then move toward guilt - even if the loss you are currently experiencing was completely out of your control. Guilt creates the "what if" questions and "if only" statements that focus on how the loss could have been avoided or at least altered by your involvement, even if those ideas are completely wrong and insanely unfair. Did I do something that could have put all these events into motion? Knowingly or not? Could I have changed the outcome if I just altered one thing? Said one thing differently? Stayed five minutes later? Left five minutes earlier? Sometimes we do realize that something we did could have changed the outcome or was not the "right" thing to do, and that adds guilt and stress to our process, which can put us into a depression.

The depression stage is usually described as a phase of confusion and lack of motivation as we are uncertain about what is next and how we are going to adjust to whatever we cannot predict or see in our futures. While those feelings are valid, the things we tell ourselves here are usually not - which can lead to us stuck in this phase for a very long time. The opposite of depression is play - people do not choose to play when they are in a state of depression. Play is free and involves choice, and depressed people do not choose much at this stage because they fear everything they touch will be wrong or cause another heartbreak, as well as they have little identity in this "new world" and aren't exactly sure at this moment how to navigate it.

Gradual acceptance is just that - slowly where we start to make sense of the new normal and begin to create the new rules that will provide us with some order as we move in the future. We go through this stage so we can figure out how to make the most of the situation - find the silver lining or something positive in the loss which includes what Fisher calls the "moving forwards." As you create a "new normal" and look toward a future without the lost item, you will find things that give you a new, comfortable sense of self again, things that will make you laugh again, things that will make you feel happy again. During most stages, you just need to move, not necessarily move forward, as shown in the non-linear thinking of all the grief models so far. The "moving forwards" phase is where you find more and more hope and the potential for joy as you continue the journey of processing that loss, but it will not always be an easy or smooth transition, even from the stage of gradual acceptance.

Fisher says this is capped by disillusionment, in whatever you have determined to be the system or thing responsible for your loss. If your best friend left your shared place of employment, and you are grieving that loss, you could blame the employment, which can create a sense of disappointment in your workspace, even if you hadn't had that there before, or even if it's not deserved. If we believe that this life change is against our best interest, that some contract is broken, I may want to leave too, but now I don't know how to maneuver through those feelings and find a new job, for example. That's a normal part of the transition of change, says Fisher. During this stage, you may again revert to unmotivated or lack of action, increasing your dissatisfaction with the current situation, going through the motions but not finding joy, and constantly looking for how it could just be different if we left too.

Similar to depression, this phase of disillusionment can also lead to hostility - which can hurt any progress you have made so far in creating a "new normal" with "new rules." Not only will depression convince you that you aren't even the person you thought you were, but that this change will cause you to become a new person - and your determination to "win" at the grief comes at any cost, even losing yourself or the self you were before the loss. It is not a healthy step, necessarily, as you are willing to give up your former relationships to others and yourself to "win." During this hostility phase, we throw away our new rules or at the very least ignore them, sometimes even pretending that you don't need anything new after all.

Denial is sandwiched between these hostility and anger phases. Anger is also part of the fear and threat that we cannot change or move through this grief. Denial creeps in as a way to avoid that change has to happen. Eventually, we find our way to gradual acceptance, which takes time and may have many forward and backward steps. Just because we find a bit of acceptance after a loss does not mean it is erased from our memories or that the pain is completely gone. It simply means that you have grown to a place where you can tolerate it, and that the pain lessens over time.

Once we then settle into the "new normal," we may find ourselves in complacency again, which Fisher says is a comfortable rotation. The endings and the beginnings are the most difficult for us, while the middle tends to be where we can go on auto-pilot and consume ourselves with other details that take more attention at the time.

Fisher's 12 steps are similar to the phases and stages of Kubler-Ross and Bowlby and Parkes, and any or all of them can help you be successful as you move inside of your grief. But there are no easy paths in the grief bubble. You have to keep moving and you have to feel all the feelings, which is no simple or comfortable task.

We are firmly in the G here of the G.R.I.T. method. There is a way forward, and as we pass through the steps and they become familiar for you, you will find ways, particularly with some losses, to move through the stages quicker and find the funny faster.

CHAPTER SEVEN

Release: The Secret Weapon

Oh, somewhere in this favoured land the sun is shining bright,
The band is playing somewhere, and somewhere hearts are light;
And somewhere men are laughing, and somewhere children shout,
But there is no joy in Mudville—mighty Casey has struck out.
                    -Casey At The Bat - Ernest Lawrence Thayer

There is often "no joy in Mudville."

As Thayer states in his 1888 poem "Casey At The Bat," the joy in the town that rested on the bat and shoulders of baseball player Casey could not be found, when despite his best efforts to hit one out of the park and win the game, Casey struck out at the plate.

Striking out comes with taking risks. We take risks in love, in careers, in relationships, in anything that stretches us outside of our comfort zones. In reality, we also don't find our comfort zones until we stretch a bit and then relax to know how far we are willing to bend. And then we sometimes break if we stretch too far.

Rubber bands often stretch to hold things together. Sometimes they break. And so do we, usually when we least expect it.

The release that comes when the rubber band breaks and shrinks back to its original or even smaller form is visible.

That can happen with us too.

When loss impacts us and we break, we can feel smaller than we were when we started the journey.

If you are out of a job, you may think you shouldn't have ever done that job in the first place - after all, look where it got you.

If you are grieving the loss of a relationship, you may think 'why did I try? Why did I put myself out there?'

If you are grieving the death of someone, you may think you were not worthy of being loved by or being in the presence of someone so great.

That's the grief providing that negative, unfair, and inaccurate self-talk. It's there, and we have to decide if we are going to listen to it. And many times, we do.

When we are in these major depressive states, the 'opposite of play' states, we do not see how any joy could ever return to Mudville. It is seemingly never-ending despair.

And then a moment of release comes. Sometimes it comes in the form of tears. So many tears.

And sometimes it comes in the form of *laughter.*

My sister was 23 and had begun her first teaching job three months prior to her accident at a small parochial school in central Illinois. She was teaching English over several grades and was assigned a group of "we hope you'll make it to graduation" seniors, a challenge for any teacher, but definitely a tough one for a first-year teacher. Kristi rose to that challenge, creating interesting and creative assignments, incentives, and connections for the students and the material to just get them to that graduation date.

As she lay in the hospital bed, my sister Julie and I knew she would want us to comfort "her kids," so we left the ICU waiting room hosting duties to our parents and headed north to be with those students.

Although for years people had mentioned our physical similarities, I did not expect them to be so triggering to the teenagers, but when I entered the room, the students gasped and cheered, thinking Kristi was walking in the room.

Within a few moments, they began to realize that I was not Kristi, and then they were all the more traumatized.

I was wrecked and heartbroken already but to think I had caused these young people even more pain in a way to comfort them was unimaginable. We quickly found our exit after I found the courage to share some encouraging words, never to return.

When she passed less than three weeks later, the school administration canceled school for the day of her funeral.

So many students and faculty members were coming to the visitation and funeral services, and I knew it could be triggering to see me and wonder how we could look so alike and yet not be their Kristi. I hid as much as possible from them to avoid causing them additional pain, and ended up having great conversations during that hiding time with many of her college friends, ones she had just recently left when she graduated five months prior.

They shared stories of her experiences, ones I had never heard before as I moved away from home to take my first job as she headed to college.

As the time of the visitation's end neared, I took note of the floral bouquets and arrangements that had been sent and noticed a large one from her college friends of white lilies. I had no idea she loved lilies so much, so I asked the group.

They told the tale, as I remember it, of a trip to a beach they had taken together, in Florida, I believe. During the trip, one suggested they all go to a nearby nude beach.

Never a person to pass up the opportunity to entertain and toss in a little sass, Kristi responded, "No way anyone is going to see my lily-white ass."

Among the hilarity of the moment, her nickname, one I never knew existed until that day, was born.

Lily is now the middle name of Julie's eldest daughter and our Pyrenees puppy, who are both lily-white.

The relief I felt in that moment, to learn something about someone I had lost, that was joyful and humorous, could have made me feel guilty. Guilty for not knowing about it ahead of time - "Did I even know her?" Guilty for laughing at a sad and sorrowful time. But instead, it was relief, hope, joy, that somehow, someday things would get better, or at least different than the despair felt at this moment.

And even after her death, I can still learn of the joy and light she brought to others.

Because "somewhere in this favored land the sun is shining bright; the band is playing somewhere, and somewhere hearts are light, and somewhere men are laughing."

Even if there is no joy in Mudville to be found on a given day or a given moment, other places, joy and laughter and light exists, and it can and will be found for us again.

CHAPTER EIGHT

Welcome to the Pity Party

Did you get an invitation to the pity party?

Or are you the one throwing it?

Part of the grieving process no matter if you're following the G.R.I.T. method, or any other, is to go through a bout of depression. Depending on the gravity of the situation, it can be for a short spurt of time or it can last for years.

It is natural, and important, and, dare I say, *required* for you to throw a small, intimate gathering I call a "pity party."

The pity party is not without rules, however, so not just *anyone* can throw or attend one at any time.

Here are the three rules:

<u>Pity Party Rule #1:</u> no guests are invited.

This is a "Pity Party for One" and while there are no doubt many others just as pitiful as you, or others you'd like to invite into your party space, YOU cannot invite them.

That does not mean they cannot join you - but joining you must be a choice they make, rather than joining you because they feel obligated to help you through this pain, because they want to share with you how they got through it, or because they told you at the early stages of this loss that you could call them at any time and they would be there, not really expecting you to do it.

Of course, this doesn't mean that if you are in desperate need of reaching out to someone, that you shouldn't call - you absolutely should. Keep in mind here that depression and pity parties are two different things.

If you or someone you know is in crisis, call the National Suicide Prevention Lifeline at 800-273-8255 or text HOME to 741741 to reach a trained counselor at the Crisis Text Line.

A pity party is a chance to wallow and to feel all the feelings in a safe, comfortable environment that allows you to do so.

You can go through all the external emotions at a pity party from throwing things in anger to eating all the things in seeking comfort.

But the invitations cannot be, "Hey, Britt, can you bring over a pint of ice cream and two spoons and sit with me?" Because we know Britt. She's on her way with TWO pints, just in case you don't like one or the other, or what you really needed was both.

Britt can come, and, if she knows you could potentially need you, she's coming anyway, but you cannot invite her.

Your people need to come because they want to and they understand the rules of the pity party.

An uninvited guest's role at the pity party is to validate, not understand; listen, not seek or give advice; share relative situations but only if they do not 'one up' the current situation, and never, under any circumstances, use the phrase 'at least.'

At leasters are people who want to appear empathetic and helpful, but fail to recognize that sympathy and empathy are two very different things.

Brene Brown says empathy allows the other person to feel the feelings, express those feelings, and brings those together who share those feelings (2017).

Sympathy is where someone wants to sugar-coat, redirect or distract you from the grief.

Sympathizers and at leasters do not think they are doing harm - at all. Sympathizers and at leasters are great people, honestly trying to help you.

I just called to tell you I broke my arm.

Oh no, which one?

My left one.

Oh, well, at least it wasn't the one you write with.

59

Notice the "at least" in that sentence? Its intention was to help distract you by showing you how things could be worse, how, although this is upsetting, you are going to get through it, but that's not really how it's delivered or how it's received when you are in the throws of losing the opportunity to use both your arms simultaneously for the next six weeks.

An empathizer would say, "Oh no, I'm so sad for you to have to go through this. How are you doing?"

The at leaster honestly believes that continuing to discuss the topic will make the injured party more depressed, sad, anxious about the situation, and that they are helping by distracting or adding that silver lining.

But when you are in the throws of a pity party, especially one thrown early, you need empathy, to be heard and validated, and you need people who want to allow you to wallow a bit at your party.

This is why invitations are not allowed.

People who show up to pity parties know what is expected of them. And they still show up.

Pity Party Rule #2: There must be an expiration date to the party.

When I was growing up, all invitations to birthday parties for my classmates had to be handed out to all classmates if they were being handed out on school grounds - to make it fair. This was a hand-written invitation, and you could usually tell when someone only invited you because they had to invite everyone as they shoved the envelope with your name scratched on the front to you in passing, rather than excitedly watching for your reaction as you opened the glitter-decorated card to see the details - the who, the what, the when, the where, the why and the how.

The when is important here. The best parties, the absolutely knock-down drag out of birthday parties went from 1 pm to QUESTION MARK.

There was no set ending - and a parent had agreed to that!

That meant as an attendee, I would have to call my mom from the landline phone at my friend's house to pick me up when I thought the party was starting to wind down, and that usually meant, never.

A birthday party in elementary school does not stop.

Over the years, parents got smarter and the ending time was no longer a question mark.

The pity party you throw, for yourself, needs to have an ending time, a deadline. The deadline does not mean, in any way, that you must be or will be healed at its conclusion.

It does mean that you will choose, at that predetermined time, to take a step. Forward.

The expiration time can be hours, days, weeks, months, whatever you need to set yourself up for a time to grieve, a time to heal, and a time to move forward.

Some situations have shorter deadlines. Some longer.

There is no penalty for ending the pity party early.

There is no penalty for even extending your deadline a bit as it nears. But you only get one extension.

Your pity party may look differently than everyone else's but the best part is - you'll never know and neither will they because you aren't invited to theirs and they aren't invited to yours.

Some events in my life haven't had the quick turnaround of a short pity party, like the 15-minute shoe debacle of 1983, but that was really when I learned that the party must end.

Pity Party Rule #3: You must forgive yourself.

By the time the pity party ends, you do not have to absolve yourself from all your sins, or perceived sins, but you must forgive yourself even just a little bit - that's what allows you to end the party and move forward, even a small step.

The forgiveness doesn't have to be fully, or even something that lasts permanently at that time. In truth, you need the practice of forgiveness.

You have been through a loss, a trauma, and while I cannot tell you how to forgive, I can tell you why you need to forgive.

You don't deserve to live in this limbo. You are worthy of forgiveness. You may have contributed to a mess - only you know that - but you are still a valuable, amazing person worthy of love, light, and happiness.

And if no one else is telling you, you need to be your own very best friend, and look into that mirror and say those words. Feel those words. You deserve to be happy. You may have made mistakes, only you know that.

But you cannot live in those mistakes forever.

You can learn from them. You can move on from them.

You need to forgive yourself and release them.

Forgiveness is not forgetting.

Read that again.

Forgiveness is not forgetting..

Forgiveness is allowing yourself to learn the lessons of the situation - to hear the new rules you will guide your life with aws you move forward from this moment.

Part of that forgiveness is finding a resolution.

Have you ever read a book or watched a movie that ended differently than how you expected it to and without the happy ending you hoped for?

Just because the book ends, and the plot or conflict has a resolution, doesn't mean it's how you hoped it would.

It's still a resolution. You need to find one to this pity party so it can end.

Your resolution is not a solution.

Let me repeat that for you.

Your resolution is not a solution.

It is a chance to move through the grief, forgive yourself, and move forward, even a tiny step.

The pity party's job is to help you move through the three steps in your grief over whatever loss you are experiencing. It is to allow you to have the time to process what has happened, to wallow in despair, to forgive yourself, and to move you forward. Its job is not to mock you or your situation. It's not.

While I speak lightly of pity parties, I may have one daily - because disappointments, opportunities for grief, and losses happen daily, my friends.

But each one has a short guest list (just me), an ending time, and forgiveness.

I deserve it.

And so do you.

CHAPTER NINE

Lessons from the Pity Party

Pity parties come in all shapes and sizes, and they are a very common and normal part of grieving for those who feel all the emotions.

Let's be honest. Pity parties bring out the devil sometimes.

When we are wallowing in despair and "what if"s and "if only"s, there isn't room for much else, I've found, except Oreos.

That sandwich cookie has been on my pity party buffet since early on, a friend and confidant. Although even the thin cookie version doesn't help with weight loss, fyi.

The pity parties that I created early on did not have ending times set initially, so in order to escape them, I had to find something funny. Thankfully, I had no idea that I had been training for these very moments.

Here are two examples of the parties I held and what lead up to their creations.

Pity Party #1

As I was finishing high school and preparing for college, I knew I was "college material" but what I didn't know was if I could afford to be "college material." I had straight A's and worked hard in all, and I was proud and prided myself in doing well in school, but I didn't think it would be something that I would be able to achieve, to go to college, because I didn't think my parents could afford it. In my vocabulary, the word *scholarship* just meant the kids that were valedictorians, and I wasn't going to be a valedictorian. Somehow my parents told me they would be able to scrape up enough money together to send me to college, so I needed to have my plan because I refused to waste their money.

In the middle of my sophomore year of high school, I was offered a part-time job at the local newspaper. I quickly fell in love with journalism and worked around the newsroom in various roles, from writing stories, to taking photos, to calling and getting court reports and sports scores. I found my passion. I was going to be a writer.

I chose an affordable state school with a journalism program and enrolled. Freshman year was a dream - coursework was tolerable in the transition from high school to university and my professors encouraged me while they challenged me.

In my sophomore English course, the professor assigned a group project - a variety of which were scheduled throughout the semester. I picked the one with the latest due date, regardless of the topic. With that still looming, I completed the first assignment for this new professor and received a D in response.

As in Dog. Not Apple on the Kindergarten chart. That's a LONG way away from A.

I had never in my life received a D on anything having to do with writing.

I was crushed.

Because I was going to be a writer. I was going to be a journalist. I was going to have my name in all of these newspapers across the globe with Associated Press or New York Times connected to it.

Who was this teacher? Who did she think she was giving me a D on a paper when I am going to be a writer? So I looked up to see her in her office hours, set times when the professor is available for walk-in visits, and I walked in. She said in 10 years she had never had a student come to her office during office hours.

"In ten years, I have never received anything below a B on a writing assignment."

She went on to mention several items she felt were not "A" material in my essay but mentioned it was still possible, depending on my group project, to get the A in her class.

I became obsessed with that group project, a presentation on Anton Chekhov's play Three Sisters. We were supposed to pick one scene from this Russian drama and present it to the class. I had little knowledge of anything Chekhov, Russia, or my group members, but I was determined to make it worthy of the desired A.

I started directing them, assigning parts and coaching them on how to say lines. We rehearsed two other times and then performed for the class.

The "cast" performed the next day, and the teacher was stone-faced, except to ask for me to come to office hours immediately after class.

I was certain that we had failed. I was going to have to retake this class because there was no way I was going to get a D in an English class in college when I was going to be a writer.

I had to rearrange my schedule, which meant my lunch plans with my roommate and friends would be missed, but I went to the office hours.

Emotions were everywhere for me - annoyed about moved plans, scared about my grade, my future.

"First of all, I don't think you're supposed to be a writer."

I was crushed.

"You should direct theatre."

My jaw hit the floor. "What?"

She said, "In all my years of teaching and education, I have never seen a funnier version of Anton Chekhov. You have a gift and should be directing theatre - comedy especially."

Three Sisters is not a funny play, it's probably not even supposed to be, but to her, I had found the humor in this play, directed my peers, and made them perform it for the class. And she was overwhelmed.

I earned the A in the class.

I was too angry to accept the compliment.

I am going to be a writer.

I am not going to be a theatre director.

I had been turned away by the theatre department at the university because I was not a major, so my feelings toward theatre came from a place of hurt and longing for acceptance, which I had previously found the theatre space to be.

I chose to participate in other areas instead - competing on the collegiate forensic team and writing for the school newspaper. I became a published author - articles here and there on hard-hitting interviews with the cafeteria staff and metermaids.

I already am a writer and will be a writer.

Who did this woman think she was?

She awarded me the A in the class for my work and I still left angry.

As I had missed my lunch date, I had no one to vent to to have somebody tell me "of course she's wrong," "what are you saying?", "how can you believe this?" and so I went through the cafeteria, picked up the green plastic tray, a plate, silverware, food and a drink. I found a spot, by myself, and slapped my things onto the table near my tray, knocking my bookbag into my drink and onto my tray. Now I'm mad *and* embarrassed. People are looking at me as I'm trying to clean up my mess. One person came over to help. I shoo her away, " I don't need your help." I'm sure I was not kind but not mean, either. Just short and curt.

When I move the things on my tray to see what I can salvage, I see, carved in block letters into the plastic of the tray, HI F*CKFACE.

Stunned.

And then, *laughter.*

From me.

I sat there, staring at this mess, of a tray, this mess of me, and this message to me from someone who did or did not mean it for me, and what does it even mean, but I just laughed. Out loud. So now my lunchtime neighbors really had to be concerned.

The relief that came from that absurdity was laughter. *What are the odds that I would get that particular tray?* And really was I acting like an F face? I don't know what an F pace is but the fact is that I had a chance to find relief at a moment where I was overwhelmed with loss.

In this case, the loss for me was loss of what I thought I was going to be. My plan was to be a writer. And to have somebody tell me I shouldn't do that was crushing. I heard "You're not good enough," rather than the desired "You're really good at this."

Since the second item was not something I cared to be good at, the compliment fell on deaf ears.

I wondered, *Why am I letting this bother me?* despite knowing myself to always be a people-pleaser. *Why am I letting one person's opinion be the answer to the rest of my life if I don't even value this person's opinion?*

So those two words and the laughter they provoked helped me to realize that moment for what it was: advice unsolicited, yet advice from someone with a bit of an eye for spotting talent. I looked at it at first as this woman doesn't know who I am , and then perhaps maybe this woman sees a different talent in me then I'm allowing myself to see.

About three months later, I changed my major from journalism to English and decided to be a teacher, teaching English, journalism, and theatre. I went on to teach English, journalism, and direct numerous high school and community theatre productions and still am. And I'm a writer, too.

Although now, I prefer to direct comedies that are supposed to be comedies - and I look to find the funny and accentuate it in almost everything.

Pity Party #2

I became that teacher and then found my first job in a tiny northern Illinois town, which had a single theatre production each year. My home high school had not been that much bigger but had five year-round productions, and I thought I could do it all - just had to start building.

So I started finding students with minimal interest and convincing them they could, we could, add more theatre experiences to their school.

In addition, I was teaching my own classroom for the first time and found that using my humor and wit could help me not only connect with students as their teacher, but also discipline in the classroom.

I'm not exactly sure what transpired but from what I heard, students liked me, enjoyed attending my class for the most part, and sometimes in administration, that raises red flags.

One day, after a long teaching day and right before a long rehearsal, my principal pulled me into a side room in December, near the very end of my first semester, to tell me I needed to stop being so friendly with my students and joking around with them.

I was floored. This was how I found a way to connect. I finally felt as I was myself and able to be authentically me. I guess I didn't realize that I could be a lot for some people.

I was even more offended by any suggestion that having fun in the classroom could be considered wrong or inappropriate because, god forbid, the students were enjoying learning, and that this principal had yet to spend five minutes in my actual classroom. I'm not sure if he observed me outside the classroom at rehearsals or in the halls, or if he heard reports from reliable sources, but he certainly did not have a primary source - himself.

"You'd better get it together or you're not going to last here."

I was hurt, but, as a first-year teacher hoping to retain my position, I told him I would work on it, although I wasn't really sure what "it" was, and then went to a long rehearsal where I distanced myself from the students and the work, as the conversation replayed over and over again in my mind.

I left rehearsal an angry person, who needed comfort Oreos and planned my evening pity party. I drove 15 minutes north to my apartment and, determined not to grab Oreos locally, continued driving another 30 minutes north to the "fancy" Eagle grocery store.

I shopped as if a winter storm was coming through - too much of everything, hoarding for an apocalypse in the middle of the fear of ice and snow but may have trapped the Ingalls family in 1881. There was a bit of snow and ice on the ground but nothing justifying the massive grocery haul in my cart for a single person. Especially since there weren't necessarily "ingredients" in my cart, but rather processed junk food.

I'll show that principal, I must have told myself, *I'll just eat a bunch of junk food, gain weight, and feel horrible about myself. That'll show him!*

Flawed logic indeed, but as I checked out, spending more money than I should have on food products I didn't need nor really want, I was still angry and hurt.

I plowed my cart to the dark, nearly empty parking lot, wheels not rolling well through the ice and snow remnants of winter precipitation two days prior.

I drove the 30 minutes back to my apartment, expertly climbed the outdoor stairs to my apartment despite the icy and cold steps, and tossed everything, including the bags, into the refrigerator, and climbed into bed. I didn't even eat or unpack a single thing.

The covers were over my head when my landline phone rang. It was almost 10 p.m. Who could be calling me?

Long before caller ID existed, and in essence spam calls, I answered cautiously, still angry and hurt.

It was the grocery store. I had left my wallet in the cart in the parking lot and someone brought it inside to the clerk, where she found my driver's license and looked me up in the phone book and called my number.

It had to have been a miracle that she found me, because I had only lived in the area less than six months at this point, and how did I make it in the phone book already?

I was not gracious as I was angry now with myself AND that principal, but I asked when they closed.

"Five minutes," she replied kindly.

Knowing it's a 30-minute drive north, I then asked, "When do you open in the morning?"

"6 a.m."

"I'll be there," I muttered.

"Ok, I'll put it in the safe—"

Click. I hung up the phone before she could finish her sentence.

I realize now how much of an ungrateful brat I was being at the time. It wasn't directed at her, and I hope she didn't take it as such, but I was now enraged.

I planned my mornings, and now I had to get up even earlier, and *it was all that principal's fault!*

A 30-minute drive north, a 45-minute drive back to pass my apartment and get to school on time means I now have added almost 90 minutes of wake time to my morning for a silly mistake.

I slept angry. I woke angry.

I drove the 30 minutes north, arriving one minute prior to opening time and watched the employees enter the store as the doors were unlocked for the business day.

I marched in and went directly to the customer service desk and told the manager why I was there.

She graciously opened the safe and handed the wallet to me.

"Thank you," I muttered, peering inside and finding everything completely intact - nothing missing.

Grateful was not in my vocabulary at this moment. Although the transaction in the store had taken mere moments, I already felt the pressure of being late for school, so I quickly walked back to my car, the only close one in the parking lot as the employees took further spots to save close ones for customers.

Focused on getting to my car and getting on the road, I did not notice the snow and ice that I had pushed my cart through just over eight hours prior.

I should have.

As I approached my car, a blue Ford Escort, I slipped on the ice, falling backward and sliding, watching as if in slow motion as my feet flew underneath my car as if I was being wheeled on a gurney, and I kept going.

I reached my hands up at the last second and stopped myself from being completely underneath my car, but at this point, I realized that I was in the correct position to change the oil myself.

I looked up at the sky and just started laughing.

Thankfully, there probably weren't security cameras at that time or I would have appeared on some "funny home video" showcase where the owner of the footage would win money.

I laughed at the absurdity of the image.

I laughed at why I came there that morning.

I laughed at why I came there that night.

I laughed at how, yet again, one person's opinion of how I ran my life and my classroom were affecting everything else around me - had sent me into a spin that affected my mental AND physical health.

This had been a pity party of colossal proportions. But I hadn't followed the rules. I hadn't invited anyone else, but I had hurt others with my reactions. I hadn't set a deadline, but found it anyway. I hadn't forgiven myself or the principal either until my tailbone was cold and wet.

Laughter did not erase that I was covered in snow and ice and now had to stop and change clothes on my way to school.

Laughter did not stop however the principal felt about my teaching style or my connections with the students.

But laughter did affect my attitude, thoughts and feelings about what I felt about what he said.

I did not change course in my classroom completely, but I did make sure I was creating the correct environment.

Some students continued to love my sense of humor in the classroom and still are connected to me some 25 years later. Some never liked it and never will. It's the way it goes.

That principal left that school after that year, and, I heard, left education not long after that.

I don't know his journey, but perhaps I was stuck in the middle of his pity party.

Now that I've explained what a pity party is and two examples of my own, can you find some you've hosted, or even attended, in your own memories?

Did yours end in laughter too?

These were not monumental events that should have devastated me, but they stopped me in my tracks. They were losses that I was not prepared for.

Should I be a writer? Should I direct theatre? Should I teach high school? Should I use humor?

Those answers are all resounding yeses, but questioned me some decades ago, and you probably have some in your past too.

If you have still not moved forward from a pity party, your time is up.

The deadline is here.

The party is over.

CHAPTER TEN

What's so Funny About a Global Pandemic?

I want to go back to early 2020, find myself, and just slap her silly – tell her to take advantage of how busy she is, but to also take advantage of seeing her friends and family in person as much as possible. Because in just three months, it will all change.

But I can't.

In early 2020, COVID-19 entered our vocabulary, and may never leave it.

We all have grieved since then, in most likely different ways. Some have processed their grief. Some are continuing their grief.

Some losses were easier to handle than others.

But we all need to recognize that for the first time in our generation, this was a catastrophic change to our daily lives around the world.

We ALL suffered.

That doesn't mean that there are not lessons learned, positives that have come from this experience, or necessary changes that were made as a result of 2020 onward, but we need to see it, acknowledge it, say it.

We all suffered.

Some lost family members or friends due to the COVID-19 illness itself.

Some lost family members or friends due to the isolation as a result of the COVID-19 illness.

Some lost their entire schedule, their jobs, their senses of security, their homes, their sense of "normalcy," their childhoods, their marriages, their relationships, their freedoms.

Some lost their chances at a career change as that industry or business closed temporarily or permanently. Some lost their connections with others as they struggled with technology or went without.

Some lost their routines, their busyness, their frenetic energy that they felt kept them going.

Some gained during COVID-19, and not just weight.

Some gained new family members, even "quarantine floofs," as it became increasingly difficult to find a new puppy or kitten to adopt across the world. Some celebrated weddings and graduations in completely unique and different ways than had ever been done before.

Some court cases were decided on the internet.

Another baby boom occurred during the years that followed, but so did a divorce and moving boom.

People bought and sold homes at record speed and prices.

People sought new ways to access goods and services - via the internet, apps, and curbside deliveries.

People needed counseling, and that will continue for a very long time, to handle the abrupt changes in their schedules and their worlds. There are simply not enough amazing counselors in this world.

Personally, I think, every person should be tethered to their therapist at birth and have regularly scheduled visits as they age with the same one.

I'll say it again for the people in the back: We all struggled, and the struggles we encountered as 2020 ended and 2021 began did not necessarily dissipate. In fact, as the world grappled with returning to a "new normal," more and more changes had to be made, forcing new ways of thinking, coping strategies that may or may not have been available to be overused, and people seeking anything to help them feel better.

For many, this seeking for coping, and to relate, sent the grieving to comedy.

A record number of memes appeared online, encouraging ways we could connect through laughter even if we couldn't or didn't laugh in person.

Comedies that were popular when they originally aired on network television found even more success on streaming platforms.

Some non-"essential" (code for 'you still have to work but can work from home') employees began learning the lives of teachers, healthcare workers, and law enforcement in their own homes as they were quarantined.

Some "essential" (code for 'people NEED the services you provide so you'd better show up or else') employees learned about mandatory overtime, bonuses where a day off would have been more enjoyable, and being a teenager and making $15/hour at a grocery store is much more lucrative than attending school in person.

And the sourdough....oh, the sourdough. People loved to make sourdough during early 2020, especially as yeast was in high demand and low supply.

In 2020 alone, YouTube videos with 'sourdough' in the title amassed over 21 million views, and the American versions of the television comedy "The Office," which originally aired on NBC from 2005 to 2013 cleared over 57 billions minutes of viewing on streaming service Netflix before 2021 found the episodes moving exclusively to a different streamer - Peacock.

Many people asked why the show found "new life," including stars Brian Baumgartner, who played Kevin, and Jenna Fishcer and Angela Kinsey, Pam and Angela respectively, who both started their own podcasts dedicated to the show. Office Ladies, hosted by Fischer and Kinsey, launched in fall 2019 while Baumgartner's podcast, originally titled The Office Deep Dive with Brian Baumgartner, launched in February 2021. Both of the podcasts became immensely popular for fans, even earning the actors nominations for podcasting awards from Webby and iHeartRadio.

The actors themselves have wondered aloud what caused the fans to flock again to the comedy, as it had been available for streaming on Netflix and iTunes for years prior.

People simply found comfort in the comedy, the 'being thrown together with people you didn't choose but somehow found a way to make word' simplicity of the silliness and absurdity, which is a stress relief.

Some chose to watch comedies with others, while others chose to watch alone. Some participated in creating memes and others shared them.

What I noticed most at the onset of the quarantines and initial rise in cases was that the creatives found outlets to still create. Connection was sought and found, in different ways. From connecting on a video conferencing platform or watching a comedy on a streaming service, to taking courses online or from a packet prepared by a teacher who thought we would only be out of school for two weeks, to hanging paper hearts in your window to celebrate healthcare workers or creating a social media account to post about sourdough, creative types and the creativity in all of us found a way outside, even if we couldn't be together.

We all suffered loss. We all handled it differently. We all carried it and may still carry it differently.

Grieving these losses together, and even having individual losses during the universal pandemic, helps us by knowing others are suffering some too. Despair and depression rear their uglier-than-normal heads when we feel alone and that no one can understand.

Even if your loss felt yours and yours alone at this time, you knew others were suffering also, and while that was heartbreaking and tempting to compare other losses to our own, there was comfort in the connection and shared losses.

Even if others never talked about it openly, we knew they were also in pain.

It is remarkable that so many turned to humor as a way to process the pain without even realizing that's what they were doing.

The G.R.I.T. method was moving the grieving stage right into the next one.

Even in the midst of our pain, in our grief, we must find ways to relate to others.

Relate

CHAPTER ELEVEN

It's All Relative

If you're an overachiever, who, as an anxious person I am, then you want to get the A plus in everything from assignments, projects, and marriage, to therapy, and even in grief. I am going to be the very best griever there ever was.

But we must think about when we get the grades in school - when the project/assignment/exam is completed.

Sorry to tell you, but you do not ever "finish" grief.

It may feel smaller, or we grow around it, but it doesn't ever finish.

And it's through the other three steps of the G.R.I.T. method that you determine that not "finishing" grief will be okay.

Relating to others and their stories is the second step in the G.R.I.T. method and involves as much or as little in-person connection as you wish.

You get to control what is most comfortable for you and what is necessary depending on the gravity and severity of the loss. Some losses require a little amount of relating and others require a lot, but the best part is, finally, after being through so many phases and steps of grief, you get to have some control.

The pity party you experience in the direct throws of grief is still part of the grieving process, and much like the grief strategies, phases, and stages mentioned prior, the G.R.I.T. method is not necessarily linear. So you may find pity parties creeping back into the present, even after you felt they were long in the past. Just remember the three rules (no invitees, ending time, forgiveness) and move through them like a champion yet again.

In the Relate stage, you will seek, in whatever means is comfortable and necessary, people who have similar stories, experiences, and personalities to you and your situations.

You will find ways to engage with them and their stories or read a book that is recommended for you from a website or a friend but helps you relate to the author.

Others relate through talking to a therapist who verifies that these losses we have experienced are valid, our feelings are valid, and we are valid for feeling them.

Some may spend time with those who empathize with their situation or have been in it themselves via joining a support group, in person or online, to deal with similar types of losses.

Writing in a journal or sharing stories whenever you are ready can help also. Even if you share your stories with only yourself, revisiting that journal at a later time should give you confidence that you can not only move past those situations but find the lessons within them as well.

Social media carries some negative reviews but using it to connect with others who have been through similar losses or experiences can help others find connections or even reading others' stories there can help you. Social media can also lead some to believe everything they see as authentic when it's not always verifiable, so lurk on social media carefully.

Relating is about you - you are finding those who share similarities in your loss - ones *you* determine, as you can relate to someone's loss that is nothing like the one you're experiencing but your thinking that it does makes it so.

You are not necessarily asking the person or people you are relating to to participate. You are seeking and finding people and situations that relate to you to help you ease your pain and continue your healing from this loss.

You are doing this from an island of one - but we have to be careful about this. If we do not relate to others and their stories, we can get stuck on that island without a lifeline.

If we do not move or relate to others, we can feel the isolation, loneliness, solitude, which are completely normal stages and phases of grief. But staying in them too long can paralyze us to where we find it increasingly difficult to take that first step.

Feel all of those feelings, but we also must keep moving.

We know about the tightness in our physical muscles a morning after we have used them too much or a week after we have not used them at all. We have to retrain our physical bodies to move again without pain.

That's what you're training your brain and your emotional body to do as you process this grief and loss.

* * *

When Kristi took her first job as a teacher, she was roughly a 30-minute drive from our hometown, so after graduation, she moved home to live with my parents, right across the hallway from their bedroom.

After her death, my mom found it pretty unbearable to see her things all the time, so my stepdad enlisted our volun-told help to organize, donate, store her things out of that room pretty soon after the funeral.

Julie and I were not necessarily ready, but this was something he needed to do, so we helped.

It was not comfortable. We shed many tears. We donated things to general use. We found things to give to others who knew and loved her. We took things for ourselves. I took an orange sweatshirt because it smelled like her.

We worked for hours packing things away that my mother didn't want to see at the time, and, as it turns out, ever, and made the room into a guest room, although it would be years before it was called the Rose Room, after its adopted decor, instead of Kristi's room.

While it was an absolutely horrific end to a heartbreaking time in my life, this processing of the items, the things, of her life in some small way was my relating. I was doing this task with others who knew the extent of our grief, and we did a majority of it in silence.

But I knew who was living in it with me and we all were feeling things, even unspoken things, that were similar.

That isn't always the case with all the loss we experience. Sometimes we have to reach out to strangers, or want to reach out to strangers, to relate.

Months after Kristi's death, when I lived in New York City, I would ride the subway and see the people, just living their lives, reading newspapers, doing crossword puzzles, eating their meals, listening to music, and I wanted to shout to all of them just living their lives - "Hey, don't you even realize, my sister is dead!"

One of the reasons I continued with my plan to move to New York City even after her death was because of the looks of concern, some would say pity, I would see on the faces of those in my hometown. They no doubt meant well, as they really were just asking if we were okay, if we needed anything, but the faces that knew our history all too well were hard to escape.

So there then, in New York City, where people did not know my history, I had moments where I wanted to shout at them, to tell them, *how dare you go on with their lives when I am in such pain?*

I needed to relate to someone, but didn't *want* to reach out personally. I scoured bookstores looking for the perfect tome to ease my pain, and then 9-11 happened.

Then the entire nation and beyond was thrust into the mourning, with me, and I could relate. I hated that, had guilt over it, and yet found comfort in it. The relating is a step I needed in my recovery, in finding fewer sorrowful things in my memory and more light and lovely things.

Everyone knew about 9-11, and in a way, everyone knew my pain, my sorrow, my grief. And for a while, that was enough.

* * *

Following the G.R.I.T. method, I found myself in a haze of trying to relate to others - to stay afloat. I couldn't stay in my parents' house, even with her things packed away.

So many new experiences and adventures awaited me in New York City.

I was near the excitement and energy of this metropolis I had dreamed about for years. I had met Peggy in my senior year of college, bonding over the "Late Show with David Letterman" tshirt I had worn to class on my first day. My Peggy connection led me to NYC to be a nanny.

You never know what is going to lead you to the next step in your life, so make all the connections you can.

Sometimes you make connections with people because of the trauma or loss you share. Those shared experiences forever bond you to the others involved, even if you never see them again.

Before I went away to college at 18, I had not left the state of Illinois except for one trip over the river for a day to St. Louis.

I desperately wanted to travel and explore, but we didn't have the funds for family vacations when I was younger.

I was so excited to just be away from my hometown at a university two hours away, but I also was terrified of trying those new things, in case I would fail. This was during my days of worrying about what others thought of me to the point that I wouldn't answer questions I *knew* the answers to in class because *what if I'm wrong*?

In fact, during high school, I allowed myself to be intimidated and scared by the very thing I wanted to be involved in - speech team - or competitive forensics. I signed up but chickened out and became a groupie to all of my eventual friends who happened to be on the speech team. I got close, but not close enough to compete or even join later in my high school career.

But starting at a university where no one knew my history, I looked up the university speech team and made plans to attend the startup meeting. And then I chickened out. Again.

I had shared my dreams with my roommate prior and when she saw that I was not going to the meeting, she encouraged me to go, shoving me out the door.

I guess that was all I needed.

I went to the meeting, signed up, and competed for the next two years on the university speech team. I traveled to six different states to compete and thoroughly enjoyed being a part of something I had longed to belong to before.

Then I found the group BACCHUS, which stood for Boosting Alcohol Consciousness Concerning the Health of University Students - you know I love a great acronym - which is also the Roman name for Dionysus, the Greek god of fertility who later became chiefly known as the god of wine and pleasure.

I found BACCHUS at the height of its award-winning days at my university, and was drawn to the message, and the opportunity to travel.

At the first meeting, they announced the school would be attending the national assembly in Orlando, Florida, in November, and of course, they would have to spend at least one day at Disney during that trip.

I was hooked. I knew I would have to miss at least one speech tournament, but it was FLORIDA, and I had dreamed of visiting Disney like so many little girls for years. I couldn't pass up this opportunity.

They announced the cost involved, that we would be fundraising to pay as much as possible, and they were looking for drivers to offset some cost - using university vehicles but BIG ones, like Suburbans. If you drove, you could have some money shaved off your trip. I immediately volunteered and found during the trip that I quite liked driving the big vehicles loaded with young adults, but I also loved going to Florida for nearly free even more.

I did long drives, five or six hours, in caravan style with the sponsors of our trip, stopping for food and gas, but not sleep, along the way. We swapped out drivers at each stop to give us all time to rest but still make the 17-hour drive not take too much longer than 17 hours, if we could help it.

Until we hit Atlanta, Georgia. Or Marietta, GA, to be specific.

The sun was just coming up and the passengers were starting to become restless, losing their ability to sleep as the darkness faded, plus, they are young adults, and probably starving at every turn.

I was directed to follow the caravan into a Waffle House area with nearby gas stations, and as we disembarked the vehicles, the directors told us they would fill the vans up with gas and we should go ahead inside the Waffle House and order. They would join us shortly after.

We piled into the Waffle House, nearly 30 of us at once in three vehicles, and took up most of the space quickly.

I remember sitting with two students on one side of the booth, and me and Steve on the other. I didn't know much about many of the other students on tour with me, and because I was driving a large portion of the trip, I knew them even less.

Everyone knew Steve. He was tall, slender, funny, always smiling, and black, the only black student in our group of over 20 students and adults in the three vehicles.

We didn't notice right away, but the other tables that we came with had waitresses visit and take their orders, but we didn't.

We had plenty of looks in our direction, and at one point, our assigned waitress went to the payphone on the wall, dialed a number, spoke to someone, then hung up.

I was starved and tired from my latest 6-hour driving shift, and did not start putting together that we were not welcome.

Well, not all of us, but Steve was definitely not welcome in this Waffle House in Marietta, Georgia, in 1993.

My hometown didn't and still doesn't have much of a diverse population, but at university, I was thrilled to meet so many people of color, of culture, of different religions and ethnicities, that it had almost become commonplace that other places without that diversity still exist.

The privilege of being a straight white girl.

Steve knew something was not right, and started being restless in our booth. I started picking up on the cues as our directors rushed into the Waffle House.

"Let's go," one shouted to us. "All of you. Now. Get in the vans, and surround Steve."

One student complained, "We just ordered."

"Now!"

We rushed out of the booths and tables and ran out of the building and into the vans, surrounding Steve like a pack of elephants with an injured one on the inside.

I was scared, my heart pounding.

And I wasn't even the reason for the retreat.

I cannot imagine what Steve felt.

Within seconds, several pickup trucks arrived in the Waffle House parking lot, with large burly men and their shotguns in hand perched in the beds of the pickups.

Our caravan peeled out of the parking lot toward the interstate and were met with two Georgia state troopers with their lights on, as the pickup trucks followed us the two miles to the interstate.

We kept Steve in the middle of the van, surrounded by scared, white young adults.

It was only two miles to get from the Waffle House to the interstate and get out of Marietta, Georgia, but it felt like hours.

The police followed the pickup trucks but never pulled them or us over.

Once we got at least a mile on the interstate, the pickups fell back and disappeared, exiting off the next ramp.

It would be several more miles before I took a breath, and I cannot imagine what Steve felt or feels to this day.

We are forever connected here, but I still cannot relate to what that moment or any other moment he has to encounter because of his skin color he endures.

He may not even remember me, but I will never forget him, how he handled this horrific incident with grace under extreme pressure, and how scared I was, when I wasn't even the target of all the hate.

The rest of the trip was uneventful, the conference was amazing, and Disney World was delightful, yet it was marred and forever stained by this unforgettable moment on an early morning in November 1993.

I have thought many times over the last nearly 30 years about Steve and how we could not relate to what he was going through, or since.

The G.R.I.T. method encourages us to relate to others, but that's not about *them*. It's about *us*.

Steve needed to find someone to relate with after this incident, and I hope he found it so he could process his feelings about that incident, and potentially many more.

Although I was present for this incident, it really isn't my trauma that's important.

What I do know is that it changed my life, opened my eyes to how much hate there could be, and encouraged me to instead be a beacon of joy to those around me.

The G.R.I.T. method helps us all process our own traumas and find ways to move forward and find the funny faster, even when things aren't and can never be funny.

CHAPTER TWELVE

It's Okay to Find Funny

Two days before Halloween 2001, I got a call on my cell phone from the audience bookers for The Late Show with David Letterman. They had tickets for his show if I was available on Halloween night for a taping.

I knew I would need the family I was working for to come home early so I could leave the house early enough to get into the city, so I needed a favor. I explained why NYC and Letterman were my two favorite things in the same space, and they quickly made plans to accommodate my request.

This, of course, meant three things: 1) I worked for amazing people; 2) David personally would become my new best friend; and 3) it was okay to laugh again.

Just 18 days after lower Manhattan was renamed Ground Zero, on September 29, 2001, Saturday Night Live, famously known for being live on air, a rarity in television since the 1970s, and for being from New York City, returned to the airwaves with a tribute to first responders led by then-NYC-mayor Rudy Guiliani. SNL producer Loren Michaels asked Guiliani to address the audience, saying "in bad times, people turn to the show."

Guiliani spoke directly to the cameras, flanked by members of the FDNY, NYPD and Port Authority Police as well as their commissioners. He said that New York City had been deemed a hero, but that the people around him, with their jackets still full of soot from the towers, were the real heroes.

Paul Simon performed "The Boxer," live on air, with lyrics that mention the boxer's challenges to leave home and try a new path, saying "I am leaving, but the fighter still remains," and "It isn't strange after changes upon changes/ We are more or less the same/ After changes we are more or less the same."

Michaels selected this song from Simon's catalog because of those lyrics, hoping to unify and comfort a hurting nation and world.

Then Michaels asked Guiliani for permission to bring comedy back to television, in a world where many thought there would not be laughter again, despite its desperate need.

"Can we be funny?" Michaels asked.

Guiliani responded, completely straight. "Why start now?"

In the crowd and around the world, a collective relief of held breath could be heard and/or felt. That was the permission people needed to return to some of the normal day-to-day things we had enjoyed on September 10th.

But not everyone is ready 18 days after a tragedy, and that's okay.

What this episode of SNL provided was a way for those who were seeking to relate to others going through similar loss. And if they were ready for it, a chance to laugh at something or listen to information about anything other than 9-11 and attacks and fear.

So when the chance to see my David Letterman in person and post-9-11 meant comedy was okay to do again, I was thrilled at the opportunity.

I didn't know many people other than the family I was living with, and at the time, I wasn't in a mindframe to make quick friends, even though 17 million people in Manhattan alone gave me at least a few options. So I took my two tickets and just went by myself.

Because I was alone, they used me as a seat filler, meaning I could go on the main floor, in row six, instead of in the balcony where the others who arrived with me who had two tickets and two people were sent.

The show began and Letterman did his traditional monologue, top ten list, and welcomed guests, including Halloween trick-or-treaters.

The audience and I laughed, and even shed a few tears together. But we did it together, even if we didn't realize we did.

I was able to relate to the audience around me because I knew we were all going through one of the worst times in history, and one of the worst times to be a New Yorker, which I now considered myself to be.

Not many, or any, tourists were coming to town, so this audience was legitimately New Yorkers.

We completely related to wondering if we could laugh again, if we could return to our normal routines again, if we should, if we deserved to go on when so many didn't or couldn't, if we could handle all the additional scares and anthrax warnings and threats of continuing violence, if we could stomach Penn Station continuously flanked by National Guard soldiers, if we could stomach walking the streets past the thousands of missing posters and makeshift memorials to those missing and lost.

This shared comedy gave so many people the ability to think about other instances of moving forward despite grief.

The permission to feel is not one we give ourselves often, especially if we are busy, motivated, contributing members of society (even if the society is just inside our households). We busy ourselves with tasks and errands and other peoples' wishes and desires.

We grieve, relate, invest and transform through feelings.

Take the permission, whether or not you feel worthy.

Find the things you connect with, relate to, to share in your grief. You'll also find you'll share in the laughter too, and that's all the better.

* * *

Shortly after I got the call for Letterman, I signed up for visiting other shows: Live with Regis and Kelly, the Rosie O'Donnell Show, The View, Who Wants to Be A Millionaire, Saturday Night Live.

I won the lottery for tickets to see The Rosie O'Donnell Show taping less than a week later, on November 6, 2001, and went alone again, providing me with the opportunity to sit closer to the front. I wore a bright green Rydell High tshirt, as Rosie had starred on Broadway previously in Grease! and I thought that could get me noticed, but also so I could see myself in the audience when the show aired more easily.

I cried when Rosie came out - one of my heroes, as I too was a larger girl hoping for the Hollywood spotlight in some way, and had dreamed of one day hosting my own talk show. I also loved that a woman could host one successfully - as not many before her had.

Rosie was energetic, funny, engaging, inspiring, and an extrovert on camera. She was warm and welcoming with her first guest, Katie Couric, and they spoke of fun and not-so-fun things as Katie had been on camera with NBC's "The Today Show" co-host Matt Lauer when 9-11 happened.

They spoke of the way NYC had changed but had also come together. It was as light-hearted as it could be while also being reverent to the gravity of the devastation.

At the commercial break, after Katie was escorted backstage, Rosie sat in silence, in reverence it seemed, for moments, minutes.

Audience members shouted positive thoughts, her lines from movies, hellos to her, and she ignored and declined.

She had previously spoken quite honestly about her struggles with depression and anxiety in a post-Columbine world. That 1999 school shooting in Colorado rocked the nation and world as two students gunned down 12 students and one teacher before killing themselves. While this was not the first school shooting in America, it was also definitely not the last, and this weighed heavily on Rosie to the point she began taking medication herself, another viable option for healing.

I related then and still do to Rosie, although we still have not met in person. Her honesty about her struggles, and even seeing her during the commercial breaks during that taping, were things I could relate to, and gave me the authenticity I needed to see and feel.

It's okay to not be okay.

It's okay for others to know you're not okay.

You don't have to be okay every moment of the day.

And even when you look like you're okay one minute, you don't have to be okay the next.

I may not agree with anyone's complete set of politics and viewpoints - that's also what keeps it interesting to connect with others, for our differences - but at that moment, I could relate to what Rosie was feeling and sharing with the public and private audiences, at least the 200 or so in the studio that day.

And that was healing.

What I want to make abundantly clear in this book is that not everything is funny. I'm not saying every bit of your trauma can be consoled or turned into a joke. It simply cannot be.

We have to honor the trauma, express the feelings, and really feel them. And we have to relate to others what we are going through without feeling that we are burdening them with our admissions.

The stigma surrounding support for mental health is diminishing but it's still years away from providing the personnel and the funding it needs.

Rosie was the first person, celebrity or otherwise, who I ever heard discuss seeing a therapist on a regular basis.

Rosie didn't "look crazy," as many times television or movies or household discussions would lead someone to believe are the only ones who benefit from taking care of their mental health.

For some, it's an expense; for others, it's a necessity.

I joke that parents of newborns should be gifted two things at birth - the baby's birth certificate and the contact information for that baby's mental health therapist.

Everyone should be assigned a therapist at birth. Someone not in your inner circle who you share your internal struggles with, who cares for them, asks you the right questions to help you process your thinking, and one worthy of being in your corner without crossing any professional boundaries.

Of course, there are therapists who do not mesh with you, and you'll have to find the right fit - just like with any situation.

You may need a great coach to get you to the major leagues or the next level, or a teacher to prepare you for the Ivy League university you have your heart set on, or a mentor to propel you to the next amazing acquisition, or a doctor to diagnose and monitor your health.

The right one is out there - and it may take a bit to find. It would be so much easier if they were just assigned to you at birth.

If you break your arm, no one questions if you should see a doctor or take pain medication, but some believe when you're not feeling right emotionally, others will question seeing a therapist or taking medication. The stigma is shrinking, but it's still there.

The pandemic shed more spotlights on our mental health crisis, and online support provided access for people who never knew it existed before. I'm hopeful the change is one that will stay, the stigma will continue to lessen, and those who provide help and those who seek it will increase.

It's okay to need help, and it's okay to talk about mental health.

Rosie was quite the teacher at a time I needed it most, but it wasn't all serious.

During the same episode, I experienced thrilling highs.

I was thrilled to learn that one of my favorite performers of all time was going to be a guest - Barry Manilow.

Yes, I may lose you here.

I am Jennifer Keith, and I am a Fanilow.

My mother raised us on a variety of music from Elvis Presley to Barry Manilow to country group Alabama to Broadway showtunes and just about everyone in between, but she loved 50-60s doowop and rock and roll. I continue to this day to have an eclectic collection of music faves, but not many top Barry.

I've been privileged now to see him in concert a few times, but this was my first.

I sobbed when Barry came out to sing. A dream materialized in front of me.

The release of the tears both times, in joy for seeing Rosie and Barry in person, as well as the sorrow of relating to the sorrow of others, was healing, helping me process my grief and still move, even if not forward just yet.

New Yorkers were told that tourists weren't coming into the city like they used to, and tourism was struggling. They needed the locals to step up, spend some money in Manhattan, spread the wealth around until the world felt safe enough to visit NYC again.

I would certainly oblige.

The family I worked for made arrangements when they needed to so I could attend the tapings and I worked around their schedule for the rest.

I was finding ways in my grief to relate and to connect to the stories I was seeing and hearing on the stage, in the shows, performed in front of me. I probably read books also at that time, but I was finding the ways I could relate - with strangers and their stories in performance art.

I even saw it in real people who were performing.

I went to see a different Broadway show at least weekly, amassing over 60 over the next 10 months, almost all of them reduced ticket prices or last minute purchases at the door or at the TKTS booth in Times Square where you can get same-day theatre tickets.

As I was just shopping for one seat at a time, I ended up with great seats, sometimes in the front several rows, at very affordable prices.

I also didn't have to worry about paying to live in NYC as my job covered my room and board, which meant the bulk of my salary could be used, not *should* be used, for entertainment.

I saw over 100 movies as well that were either independently made or studio blockbusters on their opening release days, soaking in all the opportunities to be immersed in a metropolitan area that focused on entertainment, the field I thought I'd be in someday.

I took notes on performances in both film and theatre on how things were done behind the scenes or could have been done differently. I was a critic with no audience other than myself.

And then, I got the call that would be my "big break," to see what life was really like on a film set.

Having done theatre for years, I knew it would be a "hurry up and wait" situation with getting all the lights, cameras, set pieces, costumes, makeup, hair, talent, microphones and more set before you even begin filming, but I had yet to experience it myself.

I was selected to be an extra, now "background performer," on the set of Adam Sandler's film "Anger Management," which was filming for four nights at Yankee Stadium.

We prepared to film from 9 pm to 4 am. The company in charge of the extra talent offered food, drink, experience, and raffles for the 80 of us who stuck through the four days of filming.

Prepared for the monotony of sitting around and waiting until the four seconds we are needed, I packed extra snacks, a book to read, my discman, and my notebook. Remember, these days were not smartphone days in 2001. They were flip-phones-at-best-unless-you-were-a-lawyer -and-had-a-Blackberry days.

I was in the minority of prepared folks, and several left early after the initial excitement of "being on a movie set" wore off and the evening of setting up and resetting up stretched out.

I took copious notes on how things were being handled, who was responsible for what, the actors and notes, what I could observe, hear, feel, all of it.

After all, I was studying for a future profession, I assured myself.

The assistant directors moved us around the stadium after we signed waivers that they could "duplicate" us with CGI, computer-generated imagery, to make it look like there were thousands of us in a packed stadium, when in longer shots, there were less than 50 of us, propped between cardboard cutouts of people. We were given the instructions to make the cardboard move with our arms outstretched, with the hope that the background image showed a blur of "fans" at the fictitious game with its movement.

I was thrilled to be a part of movie-history, even as the sun tried to creep out of the darkness and I knew I would be late for work if I didn't leave immediately.

On the final day of shooting, fewer people showed up and the deadlines neared all the closer. Our last shot was of Adam Sandler running up the stairs through the crowd to kiss Marisa Tomei at the top of the bleachers.

They told us where they had positioned the cameras, one from the ground, one from the balcony overhang, and one at Marisa's shoulders. We only had one chance to get this right as the sun was coming up, potentially ruining the take with the lighting changes.

They asked us to not look at the cameras.

Everyone else obliged, but I was overwhelmed with the movie-making process, and looked directly at the balcony camera during that final shot. I really didn't mean to - and I realize that doesn't change things.

Thankfully, I was far enough away from the process that they didn't reshoot, but when the film released in 2003, I saw myself on the big screen making that blunder, and I laughed.

That experience was enjoyable because it was a distraction, I knew I was helping the filming community and learning at the same time, and it was an escape from the constant pain I and others were feeling. For NYC, and across the country, we were continuing to move, creating new things in the middle of sadness and sorrow, and helping to launch the career of Adam Sandler.

I think he's done okay for himself.

I still haven't received any thank you card though.

*Note: I've added the scene to my website if you want to catch my 2 seconds of fame - jenniferjkeith.com - under "Blog."

As you work through some of your trauma, loss, and memories, how were you relating to situations and others around you?

Were you seeking out others who had experienced similar situations?

Were you finding solitude in others' words?

Are you seeking to connect to others?

CHAPTER THIRTEEN

Connect For You

I love playing the Hasbro game Connect 4.

It isn't difficult to play. Two colored tokens, traditionally red and yellow, and a seven-column, six-row vertically suspended grid.

The player's job is to line up four of my colored discs in a row before the other player.

The Milton Bradley company first sold the game in 1974, so we are the same age.

What I love about Connect 4 is its simplicity and that even in its simplicity, it can be challenging. I cannot predict or control where the other player drops their tokens, but because of those decisions, I have to adjust and strategize for my next move.

I also have to find a connection between the pieces I have to form a line.

That is not easy, in the game, or in life.

In fact, getting all the pieces to line up when you are in competition is tricky - causes anxiety, wondering what you can do right and avoid doing wrong, what the opposition is doing right and how you can take advantage of any missteps.

In the last chapter, we talked about relating - that's a one-way relationship - you to something else.

This chapter is about connection - that's a two-way relationship, the step beyond relating. It's still a part of the R (Relate) in the G.R.I.T. method, but it takes it to a higher level.

After you have processed the loss enough to see beyond yourself, to not yell at random strangers on the subway on a regular basis about how you have suffered loss, you're ready to do some connecting.

This is when you want to spend time with someone else, and not just expressing yourself, throwing a pity party, or talking about your feelings alone. You want to engage with others, to equally discuss what is going on in their lives, how they are processing their losses.

Certainly, you will continue to relate, but this connection is even stronger.

You can connect even with someone funny in order to find the humor in situations, related to the situation you're grieving or not, in order to move forward.

In this connection phase, we're not asking anyone else to heal us; we are finally admitting that we have the power and responsibility to heal ourselves, or at least take the ownership of it. That does not mean we have to do it alone. We can and should ask for assistance. We want you to reach out and grab on to a lifeline, anything that will help pull you up out of that dark space.

This connection phase is where you admit that you're ready to help yourself move up and out and not wait for Prince Charming or Superman or Wonder Woman to come save you.

When you play Connect 4, you may be waiting for the opponent to make a misstep that you can take advantage of, but you're not going to quit, throw the entire game and all the tokens across the room, and walk away.

You may have done that when you were younger, like last week, but today, you're stronger and you know you're responsible for your own future here.

You know that tossing the game doesn't let you win - and you want to win here.

Winning here is making those connections, not cheating or having the work done for you by someone else. We are seeking good, healthy connections to help us through this phase.

Many create unhealthy connections, to avoid feeling, but convince themselves they are comforting themselves - with food, drugs, sex, social media, negativity, and more.

Those may be comforting at the time, but they are temporary, not long lasting, and more harmful than helpful to your success and survival of this and every future stage.

Doesn't mean they aren't tempting. I myself have done the Oreo Walk-Of-Shame too many times to count.

Those unhealthy connections are false, because the intention of seeking those types of relationships is to avoid feeling the feelings, and as you process your grief, you know all too well that you cannot process what you cannot feel.

It's not fun, or painless, but it's true.

The connections that we want to make are two-sided, and, ideally, are not only surrounding the loss you have in common or use for the initial connection.

If you are connecting with someone else, they are also connecting with you. Your shared experiences or losses may be the first step in finding someone you connect with.

When I shared in a small group about my miscarriage in 2008, so many women shared they had also suffered from losing a baby. I had no idea. That sharing was vulnerable and scary, but also enabled me to find connections where I didn't know they could be.

Some share in support groups and find common ground there. Some share with a therapist and make that connection with someone who has knowledge about how we process loss but will also contribute to your health.

You may connect with people who have no knowledge of your loss but you are finding new connections through shared love in music, art, writing, theatre, dance, and other creative spaces.

You may connect with people who share your love of exercise, nature, quilting, building LEGO, whatever hobby or activity brings you joy. No one in the room (or online chat space) even needs to know the backstory.

Here what is most important is making and sustaining those connections. You are building your support network for now and the future.

This may be a slow process to find meaningful and healthy connections. And that's okay.

Remember, connections aren't as much about finding people who "like" us as much as they are finding those who feel better when you're around and who make you feel better when they are around you. It's a win-win situation.

If you look to those who only "like" you, you may be setting yourself up for a new loss if they choose sometime they no longer like you. But if you no longer feel better when you're with someone you had previously made a connection with or realize the connection you made has turned from healthy and supportive to not, you can move on without that connection and more easily find a new one.

Mindwise author Nicholas Epley says there are four ways to make that connection we all want.

1. Be the same person around everyone. When we are the same person no matter the group, we feel more authentic all the time which helps us to make better connections.

2. Inspire others by your passionate belief in their best talent and then prove it. If you want the best cheerleaders to support you, you have to be a great cheerleader as well.

3. Think before you speak. The T.H.I.N.K. acronym suggests you ask the five questions before doing offering anything new to the conversation:

   1. Is it true?
   2. Is it helpful?
   3. Is it important?
   4. Is it necessary?
   5. Is it kind?

4. When someone shows you who they are, believe them. It's okay to move forward from a relationship that's turning a different direction than how you intended or you learn something about someone that is no longer comforting, healthy, or supportive. You are here for you first and foremost, and you're worth it.

Part of growing up is being able to be yourself - whomever that is - at work, at home, at school, with friends, with family, with colleagues. The older we get, the less likely we are to worry about how that makes someone else feel.

We are surrounding ourselves with people who cheer for us while we cheer them on. Positivity begets positivity, and we need it now more than ever.

I often tell teenagers to THINK before posting anything online - and that's also more true today than ever before. I didn't have social media in the 1980s to catalog or record my bad haircuts and poor choices. It's scary to think much of what happens today is recorded by someone somewhere and can be posted publicly shortly thereafter without context.

Embry's final point is believing who people are when they show you who they are. People reveal their personalities to us - and the volume grows. If a relationship is not benefitting you while you are benefiting it, if both of you are not driving in the same direction, it's okay to stop the relationship from continuing - and clearing any guilt from either party. It just doesn't work.

All four of these steps are about making connections - that step *after* relating to someone else.

Making these connections remind us that we are worthy and valued and valuable, and that helps that little, annoying pest imposter syndrome from staying at bay as long as possible, but she's always there.

Even in the darkest of times, it's those connections that will help you stay afloat.

* * *

Being on the set of "Anger Management," or in the audience of whatever show I was able to watch, I was relating to the stories, but also making connections with those around me.

I immersed myself in some stories of loss and learning with those other extras in the stands who were flapping cardboard cutouts in the outfield. With our hands free, we had little choice but to stay quiet or make connections. We were also socially distanced, before it was a household phrase, thus making it a more intimate setting as the next closest person was at least 20 feet away.

I saw quickly how much people struggled even in a metropolitan area with millions of people around, how we could all feel alone, as if we were on an island by ourselves.

After my year in New York City, I would return to Illinois and to the classroom eventually, somewhere I never expected to find myself again.

But I came back with a renewed sense of self and a sense to help teenagers find themselves and be comfortable in themselves far earlier than I had ever been. As if being comfortable and being a teenager is possible...

One of my efforts was to focus on gratitude. If I thought about things I was grateful for, specific things that had occurred in the previous 24 hours or so, and I named them, called them out, my focus would change on even my darkest days.

As an English teacher, I had the students write on a journal page every day. I would craft topics for discussion, sometimes related to things in class, sometimes not.

The first thing the students would do daily was to write two things for which they were grateful - specific, not repeatable things. No "food" and "family," but rather "my favorite lunch today" or "my brother drove me to school." Specific things. Once they were used for the week, they couldn't be repeated.

This challenged teenagers who are seldom in a grateful mindset to really think about things that were going "right" or "right enough" in their lives. That's important as the rest of the class period had been set with a mindful, meaningful, grateful tone.

Many students balked at the idea - it's not comfortable to think of other people and what they have done for you, and it's not comfortable to think of positives when you're in a negative frame of mind.

But most embraced it and were better for it.

I also embraced it and did it daily.

After the gratitude entries, the students would respond to a question on Mondays through Wednesdays, but on Thursdays, I called it the Jovial Journal.

They would write about a funny situation or experience they personally had, witnessed, or watched on television.

This would also put them in a frame of mind that sometimes things are funny. When they knew that each Thursday they would have to come up with a funny story to tell, they paid attention to the incongruous and absurd things in their lives more, thus hopefully reframing situations with a more positive lens.

My goal with the journal was twofold:

1. As an English teacher, I knew they needed to practice the language, formal writing as informally as possible as often as possible.

2. Force their minds to think about positive and funny situations rather than where the brain already sends an anxious teenager whose prefrontal cortex - the part that guides the person to make good decisions - doesn't fully mature for another decade.

A win-win.

They write and they practice mindful connections with gratitude and with humor.

Not every day was or is easy. That is no understatement, and grace would be given, and still is, for those who cannot find something that they can be grateful for today. Teens would write "nothing today," which was acceptable once without my intervention. If a student wrote that repeatedly on their journal sheet, I knew to intervene - and would schedule a chat with that student one-on-one or refer them to a counselor at school.

I told them and put in writing that their journals were strictly conversations with me, not shared by me with anyone except for two reasons:

1. They told me that they were hurting themselves or someone else (or planned to)

2. Someone else had hurt them

I told them, if they shared something that personal with me, they knew I was going to have to let someone with more specialized knowledge and education know, and if they were still going to share that, they wanted me to tell someone else.

It was a request for help.

I honored that, and used it multiple times over my 20 years of education behind the desk.

I actively provided a safe space for my students to land, to reach out and ask for help, or even suggest there might be something they need help with. The English teacher can do that a little more easily - through journals and expression - than other subject areas, so I dove in to be able to provide that.

It's easy to see connections are available when we search for them, but less obvious when we are in that dark space and struggling.

Have you ever been in a dark room, one that has no light at all, and closed your eyes for a second, then reopened them?

Upon reopening, the room has lost all features, the darkness is everywhere. The room feels smaller and compact and overwhelming.

If one little hint of light creeps into that darkness, a little teeny tiny bit, your eyes begin to adjust and the shapes of the objects in the room start to form.

That is exactly what happens when you seek connection and when you form them. You open your eyes and seek connection. When one begins to form, a little bit of light illuminates the room - you don't need much to show you the way out of the darkness - just a hint to locate the door.

Of course, getting up and moving toward the door is a different task altogether.

And that's one where you need to know your worth before you pick yourself off the ground.

CHAPTER FOURTEEN

Stop Scamming Yourself

You might think you wouldn't fall victim to the scams you read that are deceiving others online.

Victims of scammers aren't stupid though. They are human.

They are trusting

They have seen things. They believe what they see.

They believe people wouldn't lie to them. Even when we think it's suspicious and if we doubt a little bit of the authenticity.

Here's the truth - we fall for scams every day.

We tell ourselves untruths. We know when we say them to our reflections in the mirror that they are not true. And yet, they can alter our opinions, what we wear, how we interact with others, and even what we do that day.

The self talk can be the scam we all fall prey to from time to time or always.

To be fair, we want to have humility - never thinking so highly of ourselves that we are shocked we do not have a live feed running to millions of viewers every second of the day. God forbid.

But we also don't want the other end of the spectrum, feeling so low of ourselves that we aren't worthy of having even fifteen minutes of "good enough" footage of our day to be shared with others.

Imposter syndrome, I've heard it called.

Not good enough-itis, others weirdos call it. (It's me, okay. I'm a weirdo.)

Imposter syndrome may not be the right word or term, but even on days when I really feel the "I did good things today," or "I'm feeling pretty good right now," or even "my hair is having a day!" I convince myself otherwise because I find limitations to it - the buts.

"Yes, I did good things today, but not enough of them," "but not fast enough," "but not what I expected to do so my list is still a mile long,"

That word.

Enough.

What is enough?

Even the questioning part of the process makes us think we might not be good enough.

As a parent, you worry that you're going to do some damage to your children - risk their lives before they are even born, sometimes before they are even conceived, or once they are here, living and breathing in your home. What if you do something, something completely unintentional that risks their lives, or hurts their spirits?

You worry in your job that if you don't do something perfectly that you'll be fired.

You worry when you apply that your resume will immediately be deleted, or even laughed at, because you're not even good enough for an interview.

You worry that you won't please a spouse, a friend, a coach, a teacher, a mentor, a boss, a customer, a stranger, and they won't "like" you and want to see you again.

Or you won't please them enough.

Sound familiar?

If not, you are one of the lucky ones who doesn't believe in the scams we trick ourselves with negative self-talk. Congratulations. Tell us your secrets. We won't believe them, but we will worship you in droves.

That word - enough - can become a mantra.

Many people embrace the "I've never been good enough," or "I'll never be enough" mantra instead.

In times of grief, trauma or loss, the mantra flies to the forefront.

Are you grieving enough?

Are you taking enough time for yourself?

Are you taking care of all the things you need to do well enough?

These worries can throw people into micromanaging all the details, overworking to avoid other things or to make sure that my "enough," which could appear as "extra" to others, is "enough" for the one I am trying to impress.

*I'll be more than enough. I'll be **extra** enough.*

I'll leave no stone unturned, no glass unfilled, no paper unfiled. There will be no threat that I'm not enough because I will make sure to fill up all the space.

I'll be so much enough that I'll be too much, which can even be worse, but it won't seem like it to me, because I'm so busy trying to cover that I don't feel like I'm enough, that you'll never see that - you'll see the extra as too much and then I will have made it awkward and climb deeper into my darkness until next time.

That is exhausting.

That is reality for the "never good enough"ers in the world.

During this connection phase of grieving this loss, you are trying to relate and connect to real and truthful people and experiences, but many times we are not being real and truthful to ourselves.

Do we judge others the way we just ourselves?

Whomever we want to relate to or connect to?

Are we asking if they are "good enough" or "enough" for us to connect with or relate to?

Usually not. If we find a way to relate or connect, that's it.

They are in.

They are in the inner circle...until we change circles.

Done deal.

No more questions asked.

Do you ever think you are the person others are trying to relate to or connect with?

They are finding *you* - and thinking "they are enough for me."

Maya Angelou said, "When someone shows you who they are, believe them the first time."

When people trust you with their stories and themselves, they are telling you *you are enough.*

* * *

When I started therapy for the first time several years ago, I discussed my imposter syndrome and my overachieving ways with my therapist.

I shared with her that I worried that I would never be enough or good enough, even at therapy. I needed to get the A plus, the 100%, in all the things. In fact, if I could get two plusses, that would be best.

105% A++

We laughed together, but she also knew I was serious.

She then created a small, tangible, achievable homework assignment at the end of every session. Something I could do, complete, check off my list that gave me the A++.

By the way, I realize we aren't supposed to receive grades in therapy. She eventually told me there are no report cards.

Overachievers have always loved the hierarchy of the grading system, that there is a ranking of how "enough" we are.

Some people are comfortable in the "C" range, while some are perfectly fine with the "just passing" part, and others want a new category above an A+ to strive for even more.

As COVID-19 canceled classes at so many levels of education in the spring of 2020, schools from kindergarten to the Ivy League adopted altered grading systems, many of which were pass/fail.

Some of the schools determined from then on, they would not return to the grading system they had had previously, keeping the "you either do the work, or you don't" mentality.

Satisfactory or No Credit.

Imagine if we treated our connections with others – and ourselves – the same way.

Satisfactory or No Credit.

It's enough or it isn't.

I know it's not that easy - but it could be.

My therapist knew I needed to achieve, so she gave me the homework.

She gave me the Satisfactory. Even though we both knew I was going for – and would be receiving – that A+ on my still-fictional "therapy report card."

Again, she reminded me that wasn't a thing.

I needed to invest in the best and right connections - myself.

* * *

Growing up, I longed for those "best friends since birth" that some of my acquaintances had. I thought having the largest amount of friends or people around you, wanting to be around you, showed you were "good enough" to everyone else with eyes.

Like all misguided middle schoolers, I tried to collect friends like baseball cards - finding the rare ones that no one had as well as the popular rookie cards.

I was really no good at it – because I wasn't concerned with being friends TO them, but rather to collect them.

They may say otherwise, I promise I did not pay them to, but I was still learning how to be a good friend, enough of a friend.

These days, I have best friends. Many of them. Some I have yet to meet in person. Some not even born yet perhaps.

That's not to brag - let me explain.

I think it's important to have a best friend in every city, in every situation, in every corner of your life.

They may not be your only best friend (but they could be).

The connections between my best friends are the best – at the moment they are connecting with me.

So if I travel and see a friend, they are my absolute best friend. We are connecting, we are telling stories, we are sharing our lives, meals, hotel rooms, etc. with each other. Besties forever.

And then we go back home. To our lives. And may not speak again for a while.

That's okay.

We are still best friends.

It's not a competition on who gets to be the "best" friend. You can have thousands of best friends, besties, as the kids say.

I may have best friends whom I don't speak to for a decade, but once I do, I connect with them all over again and we are best friends again at that moment.

When I have a memory of a best friend, we are best friends again.

I don't have to be in the same room, state, or state of mind with my best friend to still know they are my best friend.

And, here's the big revelation, they don't have to think of me as their best friend. Ever.

Read that again.

I don't have to register as their best friend.

They can be my best friend. But they never have to worry about putting me in that category for them.

That doesn't change our relationship. It doesn't change my hierarchy.

I know when I am with them, I'm an A+ friend, worthy of "best" status, but I'm not responsible or even allowed to force them to designate me as such.

It doesn't change my value.

It doesn't.

But here's where it counts – I am with myself every day, every minute of every day. Can't escape me. I'm there.

And I do not treat myself like I'm my own best friend.

And that's the problem.

What does best friend mean?

My best friend:

Sees me.

Helps me share it with others.

Encourages me to share.

Laughs with me.

Cries with me.

Is honest with me.

Predicts my moods.

Loves me unconditionally.

Tells me I'm worthy..

that I have value.

that I'm enough.

See, a best friend doesn't have to get all the questions right in a "Newlywed"-inspired game show, although that can be fun - knowing your favorite movie and ice cream can't beat a great best friend party.

But best friends really just have to see you, remind you of your worth, and encourage you to see it too.

To be your own best friend, you also have to learn to recognize the potential in yourself, to provide yourself with positive self-talk, to make your own connections within yourself and your memories. Even those memories that include trauma and loss.

You know those types of experiences are ripe with lessons learned, even if you haven't grasped the full curriculum of them yet.

Time and processing will help you discover those gems.

Being your own best friend means to be your own cheerleader and coach.

When you know yourself, you know how to coach yourself, to push yourself. You know what will work to motivate yourself.

Be your own biggest fan. When you find something you know you do well, continue to do it. Find a way to do it more, especially if you like it.

If you love it, find a way to make money doing it, even. You may find it lucrative and enjoyable if you're interested enough in turning it into a career or a side hustle.

Being self-aware will help you become your own best friend, not that you won't need others to be best friends in your life. But if I could have one around me all the time, I know I'd be better for it.

Making the connection with yourself can be your superpower too.

Invest

CHAPTER FIFTEEN

The Best Investment

Financial expert Suze Orman said your first memory of money can predict a lot of your future relationship with money.

If you remember not having enough of it, you'll work to have more than enough of it. If you remember having too much of it, you'll feel comfortable around it. This could be another example of why connecting money to something you love will help it grow.

Money is an investment. The term investment is usually related to money, the market, and finding ways to make more of it.

For the G.R.I.T. Method, G is Grieve, R is Relate and I is Invest.

How we spend our time, our energy, how we allow us to prepare for our future.

My first money memory that I can recall happened when I was ten. My sisters and I were shopping in a thrift store, not because we thought it was trendy and cool, but because it was affordable and necessary.

My parents had divorced over the summer, and my two sisters, mom, and I journeyed 30 miles north and moved into her childhood home, a gift from my grandmother. I was in a new town, with a new parochial school and a new dress code, which required dresses for girls.

As we wandered through the thrift store, my sisters, then 4 and 5, headed for the toys, and I headed for the entertainment section - which, in 1984, was vinyl records. I loved music. It spoke to me - expressed my feelings in ways I couldn't with words.

I am not a musician, to this day, but I am in my dreams - a singer that can fill stadiums and move people to tears with their words, and not their offkey voices; the drummer who disregards any requests from the director to lower their volume and instead feels the beat through all their hands and feet; the guitarist who can shred an electric Les Paul one second and pluck out Mary Had a Little Lamb on the violin (this last one is the man I married, more on that later).

But I love musicians. I love artists, creatives, theatre people, singers, dancers, actors, performers, lighting technicians, animators, sound mixers, and on and on - those who have found a way to express themselves, where a team can make them sound even better, and work with that team to bring the dream to fruition.

Truth be told, I love most people - especially those with talents I do not possess, but I have always been drawn to music.

It can soothe you when you are anxious, pump you up on a treadmill, build suspense during a thriller, move you to tears of joy or sorrow. What power music possesses - even instrumental.

I grabbed my "toy" of choice that day and returned to find my mother.

She had found two dresses in my size, each marked $1, and held one in each hand for my approval.

I showed her my desire on how to spend that same $1 - a gorgeous blue album, pristine, with two words on the front in white block lettering: STREISAND and SUPERMAN, a coy Barbra, smiling toward the camera in a white t-shirt, tiny shorts, and knee high socks with a Superman emblem across her chest in the center.

Mom reminded me I needed clothes for school, that I "didn't need Barbra."

I don't recall being a Barbra fan at the time, or not being a Barbra fan necessarily. I just knew I wanted the album.

And really? I didn't *need* Barbra? Everyone needs a little Barbra. They are the luckiest people in the world, right?

I'm not sure what transpired exactly, if I wore my mother down, if I resorted to tears, but I left without the two dresses and with the album that day.

I look back now and I know why I wanted it - people who are rich have things they don't need, or at least I thought that's what being rich was all about.

I started at that point collecting stuff - things I didn't need because people who had extra money had extra stuff. People who had just enough money, had just enough stuff.

And how could I be prepared without extra stuff?

This ideology would lead me for the next three decades of my life.

My mother wanted me, needed me, to invest in my future - my immediate future - by being completely clothed for my school year.

I wanted, needed, to invest in my future - to surround myself with things that were worthy of my investment of time.

I remember listening to that album over and over again.

It was three years younger than I was, seven years old at the time of our connection, and I played it on repeat until it was well worn.

Not many of her top hits were on it. In fact, it only had 10 tracks, when many records today almost double that.

Perhaps it was Barbra's vocals of Billy Joel's New York State of Mind that spoke to me all those years before I actually took the leap to move there.

Thinking back now, I wonder how much of a burden my trying to be rich was to my mother who now had to find a way to stretch the next dollars to cover other necessities.

She really didn't complain, never questioned why Barbra or that album was so important to me, and never asked me to turn it off, that I recall.

She allowed me to invest in something new in order to help me process all the changes I was facing as a result of the move, the divorce, the new city, the new school, and the new responsibilities I was embracing as the 10-year-old head of household when my mother started working outside of the home.

Investment.

How do you invest in you, especially when you aren't sure you should, or remember how?

Or when you are still suffering so?

That's not an easy step, but it is an important one.

So I'll make it as easy as I can - start with something new.

Investing in something new doesn't mean you're actively seeking the replacement for the thing you have lost or trying to fill the void that was left behind by the trauma you have suffered.

It doesn't mean it has to be something huge, a new, life-altering experience.

Folks, it can really just be a new television show to stream (an episode may be enough), a scent of body wash, or just climbing into that shower for the first time in a long time because that's all the energy you can muster after processing your loss.

It's all in the right direction.

Something new.

Something worth doing.

Something worthy of you doing it.

* * *

I built a grand piano, and it actually plays.

I have also built a typewriter, replicas of New York City, Las Vegas, London and Paris, the White House, the Statue of Liberty, and the Empire State Building. Twice.

I love LEGO and building with it.

I love that although I feel creative with the process, I also have direction and an instruction manual.

Things in LEGO make sense.

There are parts, where they are supposed to go, order.

They make sense.

I have one daughter who loves LEGO like I do - loves that it makes sense. I have one daughter who loves LEGO as she does - give her the pile but no directions and she'll build something no one has ever thought of before.

The beauty of both methods is they are both right.

I invest in both.

One daughter gets the LEGO sets, the other the big tub of randomized LEGO blocks.

Your way of investing in this phase may look different than everyone else. That's because YOU are different from everyone else.

The way you choose to pick yourself up and move forward is unique to you.

The hardest part to remember here is that YOU have to decide how, where, and what you build next.

That doesn't mean you have to commit to building a LEGO set, necessarily, but I love them and find them peaceful.

They are a time investment. Some of the smaller sets take minutes to put together while the larger ones take hours.

They are a financial investment. Some of the sets cost under $10 and some cost closer to $1000.

They are a space investment. Some of the sets can fit easily on a bookshelf while others need a table dedicated to their display.

They can be a theme investment as well. If you already collect or enjoy merchandise that is related to cars, or Harry Potter, or Titanic, you may have a set that catches your eye because of the theme it connects to.

Whatever you choose to invest your time, effort, space, energy, or money needs to be of value to you, and you alone.

Your investments may have creative outlets, or check tasks off your to-do lists.

Your investments may be completely brand new directions, or a shift in one tiny lane.

Your investments may be a switch of color, brand, texture, or fabric.

Your investments may be successful immediately.

Your investments may not be.

Your investments are still worth the risk, because you are stepping in the right direction - toward yourself and a different "normal," after your loss.

Regardless of what you choose, your investments are necessary for you to feel the hope, rebirth, renewal, optimism, energy, joy, life within you that you may have been missing for some time as you process your grief.

This is not a step you should skip.

It's not one you can skip and still find yourself.

But what if you don't feel worthy to find yourself?

Or are you afraid of what you'll find?

When you're building your LEGO plans, you may find, no matter how great the company of LEGO is (and they are!) at quality assurance and making sure all the tiny little pieces make it into the box, and how diligent you are at keeping them near you at all times while building the masterpiece, a piece goes missing.

A piece you desperately need to move on to the next section of your investment.

You face the crossroads.

Do you call the company and order a replacement to be shipped to your house and wait impatiently until it arrives?

Do you drive directly to the nearest LEGO store to demand (or even purchase) a replacement piece?

Do you see what you can do to just skip over that piece, potentially affecting the stability of the project, knowing that you will never be able to forget that it's not perfect or as it was intended?

Do you see what alternatives you have available from other sets you have built in the past?

Do you steal from the next bag of pieces so you can go ahead and move forward with this stage?

Even if it's a different color?

Even if it's a different shape?

I've done all of those options at one time or another - and very rarely, if ever, has the errant piece been missing due to the box's packaging.

All of those choices have unintended consequences as a result of their actions.

If I order the replacement, but can't wait for delivery and skip ahead, will I be able to go back to this particular spot in time and put it back in place? Or will my forging ahead create more of a mess to undo when I get there?

If I make the time to drive to the store to find the replacement, will they have one in stock that works? Will I be okay if it's not the right color? Is that the best use of my time, effort, energy, and gas?

If I skip that piece now, will the fact that it's not perfect affect how I view it for the rest of its display life?

If I take from another set, one that's completed or one that's not on display, will that affect how I then view that set?

Does all of this negotiating affect how I view this process? Does it steal joy from a potentially great investment?

Absolutely.

And is it really only about LEGO pieces? (I mean, I've been going on for pages now about them!)

Nope. It's not just about LEGO.

This process of investment can be derailed most by just one tiny little word that you have neglected through this process to completely transform.

It will get in your way like a missing LEGO brick every time.

And if you do not fix it, process it, heal it, it will pop back up and steal your joy every time you look at your new investment on display.

The word *forgive* may only be seven little letters long, but a lot of power can be found in each letter, each piece of the whole. It's part of our investment of self - and recognizing its power is imperative.

The missing piece that stops progress, eliminates joy, and blocks peace and healing is the biggest, baddest, worst, most foul F word imaginable.

CHAPTER SIXTEEN

Forgive the Mirror

Finding the perfect gift for a loved one may not be considered an investment for you - but for me, it's a superpower I possess. If it's not yours, that's okay.

The investment could be financial or energy or effort or time, but that's not what excites everyone.

For some, it's the thrill of the hunt. For others, it's the validation that they were the one that found the best thing.

For me, it's the delight in seeing someone's face light up knowing that you really were listening to them when they shared a memory or a wish long ago.

I've also been known to shop a bit for myself.

I'm the best self-gift-giver.

I always know what I want and where to find it.

It's a gift, really.

The best gift any of us can ever give ourselves, though, is FORGIVENESS.

It's one of the hardest things to give, because it means we have to feel and then let go.

Let's, first of all, remember to keep in mind that forgiving is not the same as forgetting. We are learning from these experiences, these missteps perhaps that have led us to this exact spot in our lives.

"We win or we learn" is a mantra used by many coach-friends of mine - whether they coach middle school athletics or lives, it doesn't matter.

We don't get to win all the time, and, frankly, we do not learn as much when we have an easy win. A hard fought win means at some point, we faced adversity and had to adjust the methodology or path to get to the win.

A loss means at some point, we faced adversity and had to adjust the methodology or path and still didn't get the win. Sometimes we are not in charge of the outcome at all - whether a call from a referee goes against us or not, we are still responsible for the reaction to the outcome.

While forgiveness is a part of the grieving process, it's also part of the investment process, because we cannot move forward without some release of the connection to the pain. Blame, guilt, and ownership of the reasons for the loss are those connections.

* * *

Like our expectations for our best friends, our forgiveness for others is usually more gracious than our forgiveness for ourselves.

My parents' divorce changed all our lives - and as the eldest daughter, I had the most time invested as their child. I have the most memories, and when I access them, I realize, I have very few negative memories of the first ten years, but the early divorce years were not comfortable for any of us.

My mother, who had worked at home all of my life watching others' children, was now working standard 8-hour shifts with an additional commute of one hour each way. Although we had babysitters and rides to and from school from grandparents, I named myself the surrogate mother to my sisters and tried to own a lot of those responsibilities.

As we grew, our visits with our biological father slowed and our school lives were busier with activities. Swapping children at a halfway point on a weekend became a scheduling nightmare. He remarried and had another child and her children from her previous relationships.

At the time of my sister's death, we had distant contact with him, but he came to the hospital to visit, and then was present for the visitation and the funeral. I took my emotional cues from my mother and did whatever made her comfortable during those visits with him, which, in her overwhelmed state, was to request very little of or with him.

We all grieve in different ways, and I have guilt over how those days were handled.

Soon after, I wrote a thank you letter attached with a forgiveness letter.

I thanked him for my early memories of sports and growing up on a baseball diamond, although I do not possess the skill to play the game well. I thanked him for my memories of his parents' house and their Christmas traditions, ever etched in my long-term memory bank. I thanked him for providing for my education and allowing me the space to grow up with my mother as she saw fit.

I told him that my successes would be mine, so my failures had to be mine also, and I never blamed him for anything that went wrong or sad in my life.

I forgave him for being absent more than either of us had wanted, and I welcomed him to have a relationship with me whenever it was comfortable for him to do so.

I sealed it, and sent it in the mail. I have no idea if it ever made it to its destination, if it was ever opened and read, or if it remained sealed and was thrown away.

I don't need to know.

That single piece of writing is, to this day, the most important writing I have ever done in my life.

How I felt when I mailed it was pure release, pure freedom, pure peace.

I have no responsibility on how he processes the letter or the information. I released him, allowing him free of the blame, guilt, and ownership of the reasons for the loss.

Yes, my parents' actions resulted in a life change for me, one that altered my course forever, but I really was finding that I liked who I was and who I was becoming more every day, and that couldn't have been possible without all the moments in my life that had led up to then.

Years later, he penned a lengthy email that was welcomed quickly by me and my sister, and our relationship began anew. We don't need to discuss the things in the past - because they are not in our future. I forgave, and that released *me*.

I have not forgotten any events that transpired, but forgiveness is not about forgetting. It's about releasing the pain, the blame, the guilt. It's really about you.

You are worthy of living forward and not living backward. Not forgiving is not living forward.

I have no judgment of you if you cannot bring yourself to do it just yet, or ever. I will just say that my hope for you is that you can break free for yourself of whatever is preventing you from living forward - which sometimes is you.

* * *

The number one reason why you need to live forward is you.

You are worthy of living in the now.

And for the future.

Your reasons are yours - your whys, your purposes, and sometimes we don't even know what they are until they hit us head on much later.

When we work toward forgiving ourselves, we find it a much more difficult process, but it's really quite the same - especially as we are more gracious with others than ourselves.

Remember that it's okay to feel guilty.

Read that again.

It's okay to feel guilty. To ask all the questions - the "what if"s and the "if then"s.

You must know the difference, though, between guilt and shame.

The most common type of guilt is survivor guilt, second only by Catholic/Jewish guilt, which are different but in the same level of severity, from what I understand.

Let's talk about survivor guilt.

If you're the one left behind after a major cut of jobs at the workplace, you may have guilt that you aren't the one whose job is uprooted, but you still have loss as you are uncertain about your and the company's future.

If you're the one who got out of the car moments before the accident, you may have guilt that you weren't the one injured, disrupted, or worse, but you still have loss that your life has been impacted forever.

If you're the one who was running late or forgot their camera bag on the way to the New York City's World Trade Center on a Tuesday morning in September 2001, you may have guilt that your life wasn't any more important than anyone else's yet you were saved.

After those situations, "at least"ers comfort saying things like, "God wasn't done with you yet," "There must be some BIG plans for you then," and "you must be doing something right," as if those who felt victim to fate had done something to deserve their traumatic result.

That has never sat well with me.

I think of so many, especially those lost during 9-11, who had young children, or unborn children, who weren't able to see them grow up, first responders who weren't there to save others, and so many who contribute to our world in wonderful, amazing ways who weren't able to see their impacts continue.

As if their being on time was what they had done wrong.

I know the reasoning for those "at least"ers. They are trying to comfort, and especially as they are most likely not in earshot of those who suffered the loss directly, the immediate danger for offending someone is low. Except, I was always offended to hear that.

My life is not more valuable than anyone else's.

I don't want anyone else to have sacrificed their life for me.

The beautiful thing about this world is the variety of people in it. Yes, that's also what drives us crazy, but aren't you glad someone else knows things you don't? I mean, I don't know how to fix my garbage disposal, so someone else does. Hooray.

I know how to find grammatical mistakes in marketing material, so I can help someone else who doesn't. That's the beauty of it.

I think of those wonderful skills that others possess as compliments to mine. I am purely in awe of how others' brains work and what they are capable of doing - the imagination, the automation, the gifts we are all given.

Many times when we are in the grieving part, we ignore our skills, talents, and contributions, or rather set them aside until we can find the joy that those skills, talents, and contributions award us, because that guilt makes us believe we don't deserve to have them, let alone to enjoy them.

Numerous studies have shown that survivor guilt is a symptom of PTSD, post-traumatic stress disorder, because people have distorted feelings of guilt and negative thoughts about oneself, but you do not have to have PTSD to have survivor guilt.

The feelings of helplessness, flashbacks of the traumatic event - even if you weren't present, irritability, lack of motivation, mood swings and angry outbursts, and obsessive thoughts about the event are psychological symptoms of survival guilt, while physical symptoms can manifest as changes in appetite, sleep patterns, and heart palpitations.

Coping with those symptoms may seem part of the process, and they can be, but the obsession of feeling like you just have to deal with them can lead you back to the depression stage or phase of grief, and we are here to move forward.

You must allow yourself to grieve and release the guilt you feel as being the survivor, shifting the focus to other external variables, rather than your internal ones, that led to the event without assigning blame.

Remember the difference between guilt and shame, because guilt is a common, normal feeling, where you have the feeling that you did or perceive you did something wrong. Shame is when you feel your entire person is wrong.

Guilt helps you process the grief - it's a natural part of the system. Shame is not helpful or productive and is more likely a source of destruction to yourself than anything else.

Both guilt and shame are discrete and personal. Choose wisely if you travel that road. There are fewer exits in the shame journey that tend to lead backward instead of forward.

Investment in yourself requires forgiving yourself and those around you who have wronged you, whether they know it or not.

Investment in yourself does not include ruminating on those same wrongs.

You are worthy of not retracing that well-worn path again and again.

* * *

Forgiving someone, including ourselves, does not necessarily mean they are "sorry" or regret the actions. Numerous television sitcoms have worn their scriptwriting pens out on characters who struggle with saying "I'm sorry."

From The Fonz on "Happy Days" to Angela Martin in "The Office" and thousands in between, fictional characters have grappled with saying words of accepting self-blame out loud to other characters. It's been featured on comedy shows as an opportunity for all of us to relate to the characters in a comedic way - finding humor in even the darkest of moments - and because many of us struggle with forgiving others, ourselves, and making things "right."

We real-life humans may find it easier to admit we made a mistake, but do you apologize to others?

Do you apologize to yourself?

This is the time to write those letters - to yourself. To apologize from you to you. A personal note of apology, explaining whatever you feel is the slip up, the lapse, the stumble, the gaffe you made, didn't follow through on, or step you didn't take.

You know you have compassion for others, that you forgive them when they trespass against you, but why can't you forgive yourself.

You spend every minute with yourself, and you are the hardest on you.

You don't deserve to be tortured and berated, belittled, and neglected.

This is when you take care of yourself.

When you tell yourself you are worthy of the talents, skills, and time you've been gifted to use for the betterment of those around you.

If you need to write it and even mail it to yourself, do it.

That's a letter you need to write, a letter you need to read.

Take care of yourself.

You have survived 100% of everything you have faced.

That doesn't mean you have survived it AT 100%.

It means you are a survivor and must carry on, protecting yourself and your legacy from now on.

The weight of survivor guilt is heavy, but the weight of knowing you have more to give but stopped giving it is crushing.

CHAPTER SEVENTEEN

Name It

Too many names, not enough time.

Me llamo Cristina. Me llamo Monica. Me llamo Jennifer.

In Spanish classes in high school, we could select a "Spanish name," to go by in classes, something we had a choice over. I had classmates who went by Enchilada, Taco, and Burrito. Those who picked the Spanish version of their given name - Tomas for Tom, Roberto for Robby, Julia for Julie. Some picked names they always wanted.

There's a lot of power in selecting a name, and we were awarded this gift the very first day of high school.

Whatever you selected was yours for at least a year.

At first I picked Cristina. That was Spanish I.

The next year, I selected Monica. I kept that for Spanish II to Spanish III.

By senior year, I was comfortable with Jennifer, and have been ever since.

Finding new ways to invest in yourself and your future is like trying on a new Spanish name. Something you, at first, may not spend much time or thought selecting, wearing it around a little, seeing how it fits you and your personality, and then selecting a new, new something.

Walking a different path than you used to do or one you are told you should follow is risky - sometimes for your ego, sometimes for others'.

In 1984, I switched schools over the summer, and all of a sudden at my new school, we had computers - Apple IIe. They took floppy disks about the size of a dinner plate and very fragile, but I was enthralled - not only with Oregon Trail, but with the possibilities of what could be done with computers.

That fall, I heard again and again from my job-hunting-for-the-first-time-in-10-years mother, skills were required at every job - something she feared she didn't have without a completed bachelor's degree, but ultimately had in spades. What she did not have was confidence.

I observed and retained that self-talk and took a personal oath in never being without skills, marketable, employable skills. I probably overdid it, to be honest, but I never had to worry about my backup plans being used because I had about 40 backup plans.

In grades 5-8, we had limited contact with computers, but still some contact. What I also learned during that time was that very few people knew how to fix computers. If someone messed up a floppy disk or a programming glitch occurred, not many technology professionals were available to check it out, so we were not encouraged to play around for fear the computer would be out of commission for others to use.

I desperately wanted to find out how those computers worked, but instead I took copious mental notes of their shapes, capabilities, and range of uses.

I was shocked when I arrived at the high school level four years later to see very few computers in the school, having assumed things would only grow in the future.

As a freshman, I had marked the "college-preparatory" track for coursework, but I really doubted we would have the means for me to go to college financially or otherwise. My mother hadn't finished her bachelor's, and I had doubts I would be able to go away to school, but nonetheless, I was taking both Algebra and Geometry at the same time, so the school was reassured my checkmark was accurate.

When I turned in my course selections for sophomore year, the guidance counselor brought me into his office.

"You are planning to go to college, right?"

"I hope so," I answered.

"Do you want to be a secretary?"

"I don't know. Maybe. Why?"

"You signed up for typing. That's a secretary course."

"Oh, I see the confusion. We don't have computers here and that's the closest thing to a computer class. It has the same keyboard," I explained, hoping my rationale would be sufficient to keep me in the class.

"Ok," he reluctantly agreed. "We don't have anyone else in the college-prep track taking it."

And he was right.

I didn't care.

I practiced every day my sophomore year. We didn't have a typewriter or computer at home in 1989, but I pretended every surface was a typewriter, and I typed all the talking around me, silently, on my lap, the desktop, the lunch table. I even memorized where the backspace was and corrected my "errors" as I made them.

By the end of the semester, I could type over 120 words per minute, which is great for anyone, secretary or college-bound student alike.

That skill led me to almost every job, which led me to a four-year university, which led me to a career, which led me to owning my own business, a degree in technology, and a doctorate in online learning.

I was told it wasn't for me. That I had picked a path that was incongruous with the actions I wanted.

I saw the path ahead differently, and stuck to it.

Robert Frost's "The Road Not Taken" is one of my favorite poems:

"Two roads diverged in a wood, and I –
I took the one less traveled by,
And that has made all the difference."

There were plenty of other times when I let someone else guide, alter, or dictate my plans, but on this one, I was adamant, and that has made all the difference.

* * *

Investing in yourself means sometimes taking the road few others have traveled before - which is risky. Very few have the answers we seek - how does it end? Is it going to be okay? Am I going to be okay?

It is possible that you will suffer loss taking this path too.

It's a risk that you'll come out at the exact same place or worse after you try the new path.

There is also a risk that it won't end up with loss; it can end with a win or at least it can be funny.

Murphy's law of anything that can go wrong will go wrong could be twisted to be anything that can go wrong can be funny.

My mom believed in funny.

She more often than not found a way to find the fun or humorous side of situations.

She loved to host parties, gatherings, hangouts. She loved to feed people with food, love, and laughter.

Each year, as the holiday season approached, we would start stocking our baking shelves with staples - flour, sugar, vanilla, butter by the pound. These were the days before big box stores that sold to regular customers in bulk.

We bought the generic brands of all things, but together, with time-tested recipes in books covered in flour and vanilla stains, we would make them seem like the richest creations ever.

We wouldn't just double a recipe. Not even quadruple. We had huge Tupperware bowls - nearly industrial size - and we would take the recipe times 10. Cookies, candies, quick breads. Those were gifts we could afford to give to teachers, coaches, friends, relatives, neighbors, and even surprise gift-givers we didn't expect but shall not leave our house empty handed.

We would plan our attack, several days a season, leading up to the actual baking day. We would enlist friends when we were kids, and when we had our own.

The eyes on our friends would bug out when we said, "Oh, yeah, we take that recipe times 10," and they tried to multiply 2 ½ cups of flour by 10 quickly in their head.

We would make some dough ahead of time because so many recipes called for rolling into ball-shaped morsels for dipping in chocolate.

Our house, as she always wanted it to be, was the place where a lot of my friends didn't just come to hang out with me, but also to be around my mom.

She would melt chocolate in the crock pot all day to keep warm for all the dipping. She would teach us techniques, card tables with wax paper coverings littering the dining room and living room just outside the kitchen.

On one particular baking day, she even engaged in a melted chocolate "fight" with a friend, spoons flinging chocolate wielded by 12-year-old Brittnie and my 32-year-old mom. My mom won. She had great aim and evidently a lot of experience.

She was born in the early 1950s with the given name Gabrielle, going by the name "Gay," a popular, somewhat common name in the 1950s and early 1960s in America. The name's use sharply declined in the mid-to-late 1960s.

My mother could have changed her name or decided to go by Gabrielle instead. Always an ally to the LGBTQIA+ community, she wouldn't dream of distancing herself from them for silly reasons. In fact, she'd be honored to be a part of their coalition. She entertained with her name, rather than being embarrassed or self-conscious of it.

She was the life of any party and loved to be included.

Even in the darkest of moments, my mom could find the fun, the way to invest in others by feeding them, with literal food, or the joys and laughter of life.

* * *

At the age of 62, she suffered a stroke and had her abilities to walk, talk, and control her right side stolen from her. She was confined to a hospital bed or wheelchair the rest of her life.

When my sister and I arrived at her bedside, we joked with her, trying to get her to speak or even sing, as speaking and singing use different parts of the brain and different muscle groups.

She sang "Wells Fargo Wagon," from the musical "The Music Man," and the theme song to "The Golden Girls," among others, as best she could.

At the time of her stroke, I was working full-time as a high school English teacher, directing the fall play, coaching the speech forensics team, married to a husband whose self-employed business was growing, mothering my two girls, aged 10 and 5, and just moved to a new home. My mother needed round-the-clock care, and I knew I couldn't provide that personally - I didn't know enough to be able to help - she needed a professional, but I would do anything for her.

So, I began to fight for her.

She needed someone capable of managing her financial affairs and her medical decisions, as she had done for Kristi during that horrific time in 2001.

Although our relationship had hit a bump, she was and always will be my mom and needed me, asking for me to step in and be her guardian.

Over the next 18 months, I would be put to the test like never before - emotionally, spiritually, financially, exhausted, hurt, debating if I was doing the right thing, justifying my decisions to people who didn't need justification and wanting to justify them for strangers who didn't deserve explanations.

I had managed my platter (not plate, platter) being full for as long as I could, over a full year, and something had to give. I needed a new outlet, one that wouldn't tax me, would give me a chance to set my own hours, which I desperately needed to handle my platter of things, including fighting in court to become my mother's guardian.

I didn't want to and couldn't give up being a mother to my girls, a wife to my amazingly*patient husband, and a daughter to my mother.

I looked at what I could negotiate. For my mental health, I decided to "fall back" on other skills in my career and left teaching.

I had been warned that my job responsibilities would be changing – increasing, rather – and I knew I didn't want to handle that as there was no open space on the platter, so I planned an exit strategy.

It included: new career options, minimal financial risk/investment, and a cushion of a paycheck through the summer months while I prepped my new adventure.

Listen – this did not mean that it was smooth sailing – that I did not tell my neighbor the very next day after I handed in my resignation letter that I was "vomit-y" about the whole thing – that I believe it would be 1000% successful from the start or ever.

However, the idea of starting something new, something "smaller" that would fit on my platter a bit more easily, something that I had control over, was exciting, manageable, and fulfilling from the start.

I could more ably manage fighting for my mother, scheduling court appointments, caring for my children, being more present in my marriage, and juggling whatever else came along in addition to monitoring and supporting my own mental health.

I had never before been to a professional therapist, but always wanted one. It was then, in the darkness where the anxiety became my means of survival, that I sought one and connected with a great support.

I have never looked back, although I still question things, still change course occasionally, still look for other roads not taken, and still make mistakes that challenge me to look in different directions and ask the real questions to get to the truth.

That is not easy.

That is, however, necessary for the growth I need to invest in myself.

After a long battle in court, I won permanent guardianship for her medical and physical decisions, and then focused on removing the source of her emotional pain. Once that was gone, she began to breathe more freely, and not soon after, went on hospice care.

She passed peacefully, without physical or emotional pain, on Valentine's Day at the age of 64. She left behind love, laughter, and light on people's faces when they speak of her. She left behind an ex-husband who doted on her, two grown daughters, six grandchildren, and more. We believe she was reunited with her Kristi on the day of love.

While those days were painful, indeed, we rejoiced in that her pain, her living the way she had been over the almost-three-years prior, without any personal freedoms, the ability to walk, eat, talk, be understood, was over.

We had to find ways to invest to heal from the trauma and loss of the past three years for all of us.

* * *

Investment at this phase, for you, does not mean that you have to be completely sold on a brand-new idea.

It may also be that you aren't sure if there's anything new, something you've never ever thought about doing before, or if even the thought of something brand new even fits in your space right now.

And that's okay.

New may just mean something that you used to do that you're no longer doing because you're in the throes of grief.

Getting up and taking a shower when you haven't had the energy, will, or desire to do so prior to the last several weeks, months, days, minutes, may be enough.

Whatever you choose does not have to be a completely foreign investment.

There are times in our lives when we connect something we love to do with someone else. When that someone else is no longer in our picture in the same way, not necessarily dead - just no longer available for a myriad of reasons: schedule change, divorce, moving, friendship change, or others - we may not want to do that thing anymore - now or ever again.

This may be a prolonged time of mourning or never again revisit that topic, restaurant, song, movie, whatever connects you to the memories of that other person. It could be a hobby or a pastime, a movie or a song. It may be too difficult and you can give yourself permission to take a break - possibly permanently - with it, if it causes you too much pain.

Taking a break can be an investment too.

I love medical dramas, cop dramas, law, order, based in reality. I probably still today watch 6-10 religiously - not always at the same time they originally air.

I connect with the mystery of it, the drama, the technology, the steamy romance, a little bit of levity, clever writing and twists and turns.

I'm certain a lot of it may not be medically accurate, but don't ruin this for me.

I've always been fascinated by things I do not know, things I do not need to know, things I do not necessarily want to know, so when you got a television series like ER, the beginning medical doctors, flashy young hot people – I'm not only in for the performance piece, I'm going to learn a lot.

In fact, if someone would just give me that prescription pad and the scalpel, I'm good to go.

Please don't.

I think I know a lot of things, but I just learned it on TV.

When we were in the ICU waiting room for 30 days in St. Louis, "ER" was ending its seventh season on NBC.

One of my favorite shows, ER had five episodes left in the season, and although I had previously watched every. single. one. I could not focus, concentrate, or view any of them.

I still loved the show, the drama, the medical information, but now, I was IN a hospital. While I wasn't the patient, the show now felt too close to home.

Just a week before, I had used "ER" and its theatrics to connect to students in Italy, and now I couldn't even allow the television to be on the channel.

It seemed too real.

I wouldn't watch it again for over 20 years, even while the great actors and technicians created amazing television, for another 8 additional seasons before closing the fictitious hospital doors in 2009.

I could have started watching it again earlier, but I had missed so much that it was easier to not start again until I could start over.

That time came in 2020, when in March, the global pandemic cleared my speaking and teaching schedule.

I found the series streaming online and settled in, from season 1, episode 1, and watched while I worked on my LEGO sets or crocheted a blanket, keeping my hands busy and not reaching for the COVID-19 snacks that were supposed to last two weeks and barely lasted two days.

I watched all 15 seasons, all 331 episodes again, she says without shame. It's not like I did it within the initial two weeks. I took my time, savoring each episode, its drama, its medical jargon, and evaluating it for what it was and is - an outstanding medical drama.

I found this love completely, all over again, years later.

While this is a simple example, fictitious at best, during this "real" thing for me, it was that movement, moving forward, reinvesting, investing in something I loved, something I had lost, that made me feel okay again.

You can find those things again, or completely new things. Either is acceptable and part of the investing of you.

Both are okay. You can find you in new, or you can find you in reinvesting in what was once you.

If it's something you loved, and it's still out there, maybe you should find your way back to it. But that's for you to say.

CHAPTER EIGHTEEN

Explore It

Investing in yourself can also look like exploring your surroundings.

Back in the days prior to GPS, there were these things called paper maps. They are lovingly referred to as the Unfoldables.

For a person who is the creative type rather than a rational type (also known as me), it's possible the map would end up in a ball tossed into the backseat of a car or left completely unfolded forever.

When you would take a road trip across several states, you would need to purchase an atlas, which was one large book of maps, roughly the size of a trunk, or one impossible-to-fold-map for every single state you're going to.

Maps were sold regularly at gas stations next to postcards and keychains, magnets and spoons, to prove you had traveled.

There is also a skill to map reading. You have to find the legend of the map, to know what color or line, shape, or objects meant on the map. What is water? What is a two-lane road?

Today, the technology exists where you can get alerts to construction, hazards on the road, even speed traps, in real time, and the map will suggest an alternate route if yours becomes congested or has an issue.

There is no map to read, necessarily - a voice can read it for you. There is definitely no map to fold when it's on your phone or dash of your car.

Either way, it's best to be prepared when you're heading on a road trip - know where you're going and how to get there, unless you're not sure where you're going and how you're getting there, until you're already there.

In 2001, post 9-11, I set out to explore without maps without GPS.

I was already taking this massive risk of moving to New York City, by myself.

During this time of exploration, I had a roundabout area in Long Island - smaller cities that were not much on maps, but I knew had places I hadn't seen before, I hadn't discovered.

For one, I grew up in landlocked Illinois, definitely not much oceanfront property there.

I wanted to spend some time discovering, so I started with a map - but I didn't bring one with me.

As a young woman traveling alone, I made sure to always have one in the trunk, the gas tank always filled, and my cell phone always charged. I also made sure to be somewhere where I knew where I was by the time dusk began to settle.

Growing up, we had to be home "when the street lights come on," so I was trained right.

I knew the first stop I had to explore - the lighthouse all the way out at the end of Montauk, Long Island, nearly 100 miles from my start, but an easy route nonetheless.

My sister Julie was always fascinated by lighthouses, collecting figurines, images, calendars, blankets, whatever had a lighthouse on it. When traveling, she finds a way to stop and see one in person if nearby.

I realized recently that I had never asked why. I just kept buying the figurines, windchimes, and more as gifts. I sought them out myself to make images to give to her.

They meant something to me, too.

Lighthouses are a beacon of hope, a sign to tell you, "you're going the right way," "I'm here," and "I'll be here."

I wasn't sure that was a shared reason, so I asked her.

She told me she had written a paper and given a speech on the topic in college, something I didn't know before I asked. (Imagine what else we don't know until we ask.)

She said, "They show you the way home. There's always someone there, waiting to direct you home, waiting for you to get home. Someone will always be there. For you. Home."

Her collection of lighthouses is her home - her knowledge that someone is waiting for her, that they are glad she's there.

My collection growing up was keychains. I would have everyone get me a keychain from wherever they were traveling, an easy-to-find, not-too-expensive-to-purchase representation of where they had visited.

I wanted to travel, see the world, the sights, take in all the knowledge. That's where I'm most comfortable - on the road.

Julie is most comfortable at home.

Makes sense.

To me, lighthouses are also freedom. You have the freedom to go anywhere you want, any direction you choose, but they will always be there to guide you home.

Think about your "home," where you find your comfort.

What does it look like to you? How do you decorate it? How do you make it yours?

That's the investment in you and your space.

* * *

I took off most weekends from the house, determined to explore as much as possible and give the family enough together-time as the parents worked long hours in the city during the week.

I was reminded that I could join in the family outings, meals, and events, but I preferred to allow them to have that time, as I knew more than ever how fleeting time was.

I had a chance to bond with the kids during the week; the parents deserve the same as they are able on the weekends.

During the weekdays, on lighter responsibility days, I could go into the city and run some errands, always having a hard stop to return home in time to get the kids from school, meet them off the bus, run them to tennis practice or horseback-riding lessons, feed them, do homework checks, and plan the next day.

Weekends were more free - having no official responsibilities and more time to explore.

I would go at least one day into the city and see entertainment, and at least one day exploring on Long Island.

I wanted to connect to my surroundings, which I assumed would be temporary unless I started making a LOT more money, as I was slowly becoming accustomed to this lifestyle.

I was finding new, even if I didn't know what I was finding.

The beautiful thing about exploring in a Ford Escort is that it's small, easy to get around, and make u-turns as I found myself in situations that didn't feel comfortable.

I wasn't necessarily sure where I was going, but I knew if I needed to, I could quickly turn around, and it got great gas mileage.

I would head off with a few snacks, a full tank of gas, and my camera. I found wonderful things to photograph.

That "island" gets its name from being surrounded by water.

I discovered some of Long Island's castles - particularly Hempstead House and Castle Gould in Sands Point, NY, the north shore of Long Island in Port Washington.

I would return frequently to Port Washington, finding something new each time to make an image of.

These weren't places that show up often in the "high society" pages like the Hamptons might, but they were comforting, calming and welcoming to me and my camera.

I witnessed a wedding shoot on the castle grounds.

The area is rich with history, more than I ever knew as the internet was still in its infancy at the time, but the stone still spoke to me.

One image I made was most impressive to my photography instructor, who told me, "If you want to be commercial, this image will sell."

I didn't, at least not then.

Maybe someday.

I gave it to some as a gift, but mostly loved just playing with the exposure in the darkroom, adjusting the shadow, how much light I let in, letting in a bit more, then a bit less.

I love having the power to control the final result - how one second could impact its exposure, the ability to evoke an emotion for whomever might see it.

I could also control who could see it, like I am now.

This image is simple in design, a downward spiral staircase. It's covered in dirt and leaves.

There is beauty in it, though, even covered in history and experience, not pristine and clean and tidy.

None of us are, you see.

There is beauty in "ordinary," there is beauty in dirt, and mess.

As I explored, I came across plenty of beautiful, clean, and pristine things.

I also came across beautiful messes.

Sometimes we have road construction that just pops up on our path, things that adjust our travel speed, time, and direction.

Sometimes we have hazards and speed checks.

I explored, at that time, and in all my times of processing trauma, because we don't ever finish processing trauma.

I explored, and wandered, and found beauty in the mess.

I explored streets and castles in Long Island, beaches and lighthouses.

I know I will never be able to travel again and be the same traveler. Robert Frost says it better when he realizes he cannot travel both paths at the same time,

"Oh, I kept the first for another day!

Yet knowing how way leads on to way,

I doubted if I should ever come back."

I cannot go back to that time in my life and redo anything. I shouldn't even wish it. We think we want to return and take all our knowledge with us, and, knowing what we know now, make different choices.

We have to remember, though, that our choices have made us who we are now, today, and what we see now, today, in the mirror is a culmination of all those choices, winning choices, learning choices, and all of those in between.

Can you imagine re-living middle school again? Ugh. It was horrible the first time. No one ever says, "6th grade was the best time of my life!" or if they do, they need more excitement.

We may make split-second decisions that alter our course, not only for ourselves but for others. We also make painfully-long decisions that have similar impacts.

Whatever you do, do it authentically, for the betterment of you and your community.

As we waited in the hospital for those 30 days to learn of Kristi's prognosis, again and again, people who came to comfort us said to my mom, "God doesn't give us anything we can't handle."

My mom, every time, responded, "I wish he didn't trust me this much."

Whatever power you believe in that created you trusts you.

If you find trouble, you'll find a way out.

You'll invest in yourself, and trust yourself, to find a new way to improve yourself, your community.

You'll find it without a map.

If you get lost, though, look for the lighthouses. They are everywhere.

They will lead you home.

* * *

Alice Walker once wrote, "Look closely at the present you are constructing. It should look like the future you are dreaming."

The problem with passion is that we feel like you have to have it all the time for one particular thing.

The good news about passion is you don't.

We can be passionate about multiple things at once.

We can lose passion for things and move on to others.

Jobs can be passions. Families can be passions. Relationships can be passions.

We can be in love with them, and then not.

It happens.

It happens more when there is stress, grief, loss, trauma involved in them, which is why, it's all the more important to find new, or rekindled, passions and investments.

The number one investment is you.

You are still here.

You may have been through horrific, indescribable pain, grief, and loss, and yet, you are still here.

I can't tell you the reason - as it's not for me to say.

I'm glad you're here.

And you need to be glad too.

So, take this as permission and kick in the butt you need to do it. Go do it.

Whatever it is that you've been thinking about doing.

The thing that you've thought, "I wonder if..."

The answer is never known until you ask, until you try. It may be no, and it may be a yes, but you won't know until you ask.

Derek Sivers, in his book "Anything You Want," discusses passions and choices we make.

He says a choice is a very clear no or a very clear yes.

In fact, it's either a "hell yeah" or it's a "no."

So many times, we say yes to too many things, and that helps us lack the passion or have room in our lives when something that creates more passion tries to come in.

So it's okay to have passion, and it's okay to not have passion for things.

All of our "yes"es come at a cost.

It can be a cost for others. If we take all the "yes, I could do that"s away from other people who would have gladly said "hell yeah" to before given the chance, our "yeah, sure"s have stolen their passions.

It can be a cost for us. Is that extra time away really necessary? Is it helpful?

For a while, when my girls were younger, I was trying to give them all the things - the toys, the clothes, the extras. I would work longer hours, doing things I liked, but would spend time away from them to make that extra money.

When my mother's stroke happened, and I knew I had to reduce something from my platter, I told my girls I was thinking about being home more and giving up my job away from home for a new something (code for "yet to be officially determined") at home.

I expected my teenager, especially, to be annoyed that I would be home more, but she surprised me, and let out a large sigh of relief, and said, "I'd really like that."

I didn't even realize that during the time I was spending time away from them to make more money for them, they really only wanted me.

After that, I have made a point to take ordinary days and make them special, one-on-one dates with the girls and special things that we share only together.

That's my passion, and I want to teach them to have their passions and never let go of them.

I spent too much time saying yes, and essentially taking something away from others who could have really enjoyed getting asked to do it, just because I could.

My girls should have a different future - one where they know their value faster and find their passions.

You should too.

What you may have learned during the slow down many people experienced in the early months of 2020 and after, things went on, life went on. Your contributions may have been missed, but things still happened.

Your contributions may be replaceable, but you are not.

You are a hell yeah.

Transform

CHAPTER NINETEEN

Humor Can Save the World

Neurohumorist Karyn Buxman has written several books with the title beginning "What's So Funny About..." and then serious topics, like operating room nurses, nursing, diabetes, and heart disease to name a few.

The truth is, there isn't much funny in the details of those topics, and she knows it.

She spent her childhood in a household revolving around medicine with her doctor father and nurse mother, and then became a nurse herself.

She knows a thing or two about medicine, and she knows a thing or two about humor.

She began her second career as a researcher studying humor and its value in medicine, and while presenting her findings to colleagues, she discovered people found joy in her presentations not only for the humor research she was sharing but also because she was funny. That launched a new career as an international speaker and presenter of information she has gleaned as a neurohumorist, where the study of the brain and how it processes humor meets the application of humor.

Her TEDx Talk claimed that humor could save the world when she recorded it in 2017, and she knows we need it now more than ever before.

My mentor, colleague, and friend Karyn knows not everyone is funny, and no one says you have to be, but you can train your brain to see the funny things.

Take, for example, this sign that was hung up on the high school stairs in the middle of the summer after the floors had been painstakingly waxed to premium shine.

While I appreciate the sentiment of not wanting anyone to mess up the floors, threatening to violate someone wasn't the intention here. But as a grammar nerd, I loved the mistake in word choice and snapped a photo quickly - who knew what would happen if you were caught doing that if they were resorting to violence for walking on the floors.

Spoiler alert - I did not walk on the floors, and I would safely bet no one else did either.

I wasn't personally being funny here, but I found the funny, I saw the funny in a difficult time.

At the time I saw this sign in our hallways, I had popped in quickly during the summer months to gather some things to work on during the end of summer and to prepare for the beginning of the school year.

My second daughter had been born 8 weeks prematurely the month before, and while she was then home from the hospital, I feared leaving her, this fragile human, before it was time and knew I would be starting that following school year in at least part-time status. Always the perfectionist, however, I wanted to create lesson plans. Even though I would be docked the money for the days I couldn't cover with my sick bank, I wanted my students to do my assignments and prepare for my classes my way. Like I said, perfectionist.

It would be something I would willingly do for free. Then. Not now, but that's another book.

As I approached the hallways (I had called ahead to make sure my hall had not been waxed - I have mad respect for the custodial staff at any location - and they are a bit scary, especially if you mess with their wax!), I saw this crime scene tape draped across the entrance to the stairwell, which was humorous enough, but then I read the sign.

I started to laugh.

I know it wasn't intended to be funny - grammar nerd alert - but I couldn't help it.

Then I snapped the picture.

Believe it or not, I did NOT cross that line - I didn't want to find out WHAT would happen for sure.

It was a great relief from a stressful time - one where I was already nervous because I had left my newborn home with her father and sister. It's not that I didn't trust he could handle it, but have I mentioned I'm a perfectionist?

Speaking of perfectionists, I've probably been one for a really long time. Even when I was younger and realized that I could wear two different shoes to school and not die of embarrassment, I learned that I didn't *like* to be embarrassed.

 I mean really who does.

Thus began my anxiety which led to my overpreparing.

You can decide for yourself if it's a healthy choice, but for me, it gets the job done.

I also don't want to be like the "common people."

I laugh because that's not reality. I am completely common in so many ways but my brain wants me to be better.

So much that that hubris leads to my ultimate fall-on-my-face moments.

My freshman year of high school, I memorized my schedule: classes, teachers, room numbers. I knew it. Rote.

I didn't need to write it down. I didn't need to have a copy of it with me. I knew it.

I went to school without it but had my number two pencils, sharpened expertly, a fresh notebook, pristine backpack ready to go.

Memorized locker combination? Check.

Worked perfectly so far.

I can do this, I reminded myself. You know I love some positive self talk.

Oh, poor 1989 Jennifer. There's self talk and there's sarcasm.

I marched to my first class and I went in. I found a seat. The female teacher smiled, but looked a bit longer at me, inquisitively with her head tilted to one side.

I ignored it, opening my fresh notebook to begin to write all the wonders of my Spanish class down on page one.

Feeling eyes on me, I look around the room. Everyone else looks like me - teenager, jeans, tshirt, but I'm the only one with a notebook.

Maybe that's why the eyes are on me, I told myself.

The teacher kindly, gently talked directly to me: "Do you know where you're supposed to be?"

"You bet," I responded, confidently.

"Are you sure?"

"Yes, Room One - Oh - Five"

"This is Room 105."

"Yes," I responded.

"What class do you think this is?"

"Spanish I?" I asked timidly.

Blink.

"Spanish is in Room 108."

I was in a behavioral disorder class which was full of lovely people, but not bilingual ones.

I collected my notebook and left quickly and I don't know that I ever looked at that room again during my time in high school.

But as fate would have it, sometimes being full circle and hilarious, 25 years later when I became the technology coordinator at the same high school, my office was assigned to Room 105. That time, I remembered where I was supposed to be and made sure I was in the right space.

The most painful part about being a perfectionist is that we really wish for control in places we will never have, and we sometimes lose it in places we should have it.

Knowing that, we need to realize that we are okay. Convincing ourselves that it's okay in that actual moment is no easy task.

* * *

When I moved home after my year in New York City, I found temporary jobs as I was searching for my next official move.

I was in my late 20s and thoroughly enjoyed my nanny-ing experience and the family I worked for. I'm still in touch to this day and the kids are both doctors, which I'm certain had to do only with my influence (not really).

I was ready for my family - the one I would create with my husband-to-be, whom I had yet to meet, so bravely I signed up on Match.com.

I had tried online dating previously, but I was horrible at it, taking dangerous risks that I should never have tried and am so lucky that I was able to walk away from. More on that in perhaps another book.

I was willing to put my profile picture online, but not to pay for the services. As if.

There were a few inquiries, but the one that stood out from the beginning was my husband-to-be, I was certain.

Funny, long-winded, detail-oriented, family-oriented, but no profile picture.

He was willing to pay to find a match but not courageous enough to put his picture out.

For that, I'm grateful.

He was a catch and someone else would have snatched him up way earlier if he had.

I was in my "late" 20s when we met, he in mid-20s.

I wish I could have found him earlier, but I know that I couldn't control that.

The year I spent in New York City, he had been assigned out of state also for work, and we both relocated back to the same area, at the same time, ready for our forever family.

It was controlled, but not by us.

From the beginning, what is attractive, exciting, and enticing about a potential partner are the differences - how we think, how we relate, how we act. As we go through our relationships, those exact things are also what frustrate, anger, and annoy us.

For both of us.

I'll be fair.

I'm not always the easiest to live with, and I'm sure all of the things I do that I *know are right*, do not feel like it to those around me.

I can't control those things in him, as he cannot control those in me. I can want him to be different or more like me. He can want me to be to different. We can influence each other but we really can't make each other do anything. And we shouldn't.

I control what I can in me, and I do the best I can to influence others.

Nothing clears that up anymore than having your first child. A child that doesn't follow a routine ALL the time, even if it's well established, unless I'm somehow the only one who got the ONE baby that finds exceptions to every rule, one who challenges every pretension and presumption I had as a childless person on what every parent should be doing.

Until I became a parent and then I saw how hard it really is.

At my first post-baby solo doctor's appointment, I took my small, fragile human in the car seat by myself.

I scoffed at any thought other than "I don't need this diaper bag. It's a quick, 15-minute weight check; everything will be perfect. I don't need all of that stuff they say you have to take when you have a baby."

Spoiler alert: I did need all that stuff. And more.

I grabbed my purse, carseat, and went into the doctor's office. Instantly, the nurses oohed and ahhed over my beautiful newborn girl, and, of course, asked me how I was feeling. Everything was sing songy and lollipops and rainbows.

The nurse led us back to the room. She unbuckled the baby from the carseat and lifted her up, exposing what we affectionately call a poopsplosion everywhere.

Runny, sticky ick was everywhere, and I mean EVERY where. In every crevice of her little body, in every crevice of the carseat. I not only had no diapers or change of clothes, but no wipes.

Oh goodness, the hubris of this first-time mama.

I remember the nurses in that doctor's office that I have been going to since I was a child did not give me a disapproving look, but rather scrambled to keep the baby warm, clean, and eventually dry.

They found wipes, and a diaper, and covered her in blankets rather than returning her to those disgusting clothes.

I threw them away, and essentially tossed my dignity in the trash too.

I know I'm supposed to prepare. I know what my brain knows, what I'm supposed to do, and, yet sometimes, our emotions are so strong that they convince the brain of other things.

The brain is such an interesting, complex, and, yet simple muscle that what we put into it – the time and effort in the practice – pays us back.

When we lead with emotion, it pays us back too, and not always in a great way.

* * *

Researchers Dr. Lee Berk and Dr. Gurinder Bains from California's Loma Linda University have studied humor for decades and have found, quite simply, that the act of laughter - or simply enjoying some humor - increases the release of endorphins and dopamine in the brain, which provides a sense of pleasure and reward.

Dr. Berk goes on to say in his 2014 study that these neurochemical changes in the brain also increase "gamma wave band frequency" which can improve memory.

Think back to one of your earliest, funniest memories and I bet you can see the setting, the costumes, the plot and even hear the scripted dialogue as clearly today as the day it happened.

According to Scientific American, the memory capacity of the average adult's human brain is reported to be the equivalent of 2.5 million gigabytes of digital memory. That's a lot. The average computer is around 250 Gigs.

2 point 5 million.

By comparison, the Internal Revenue Service, which has a massive data warehouse tracking information of over 300-million Americans and many more million businesses, holds only 1.5 million gigabytes.

My brain holds more than the IRS, but the IRS gets to hold more of my money.

So we have a massive digital library of memory at our disposal, an entire set of memory filing cabinets, and yet we find fewer and fewer memories are promoted to the front - those which are traumatic and those which are comedic.

When faced with traumatic situations, the brain areas that are involved in the stress response are the amygdala (which handles emotions), hippocampus (memory and nerves), and prefrontal cortex (decision making). Traumatic stress is connected to increased cortisol (the stress hormone) and adrenaline, which increases your heart rate and blood pressure.

Humor researcher Peter Derks said, laughter, however, involves the whole brain:

The left side of the cortex analyzes the words and structure of the joke. The brain's large frontal lobe (the one that deals with social emotional responses) becomes very active - lights up like a Christmas tree. The right hemisphere carries out the intellectual analysis required to "get" the joke or find something funny. Stimulation of the motor sections evoke physical responses to the joke. - laughter, smiling, rocking in your chair, guffawing.

Because the whole brain is active with laughter, those memories are rewarded by becoming "keepers" and move to the brain's frontal cortex memory filing cabinets.

And laughter reduces the cortisol released in your body and your blood pressure.

Traumatic events and humor are not strangers, nor are they polar opposites. In fact, we NEED a balance to keep ourselves and our brains functioning.

World-renowned relationship expert Dr. John Gottman describes the relationship between conflict and positivity as "the magic ratio of 5 to 1" - for every one negative experience, we need 5 positive experiences to balance. If this is true for our daily realities, then our memories also share that burden of balance for our brain.

Traumatic images can ruminate in the brain, negative, repetitive, prolonged, unhelpful thinking. When we are in rumination, our brains are STUCK, reliving the same moments over and over again. We are more prone to mental health and physical health problems - including depression and anxiety or heart attack and stroke.

When we relive funny moments, it eases anxiety and tension, relieves stress, boosts our immunity, decreases pain, relaxes muscles, prevents heart disease, and attracts us to others.

Humor certainly doesn't fix everything. It cannot ERASE trauma, but finding the humor in even traumatic or disappointing situations can ease the memory, even if the situation isn't funny at the time.

So even as we plan, we have to prepare ourselves for something outside of the script to occur, and that it has the potential to be memorable and funny, even if it doesn't go perfectly.

As a new mom, I looked at what was literally killing the joy - competition. I was in constant competition with not only every other mom on the planet, but also with the expectation of being the best, most perfect mom I could be.

Comparison, as we have heard, is the thief of joy, and apparently the thief of diaper bags and preparation as well.

I was so worried to be "uncommon" that I certainly fit the bill - but in the completely wrong direction.

I didn't want to carry loads and loads of useless things that "babies need" when I *knew* that babies don't NEED all that stuff.

Boy, did I ever learn that lesson.

Load up the minivan, kid, we are going through the drive thru.

I never left my house again without at least 1 million things I didn't need again. And I have the receipts to prove it.

What I am reminded of is that SOMETHING is going to go wrong, the phrase attributed to Murphy - anything that can go wrong will go wrong.

What I am here to tell you is that it's going to go wrong - it just will. But it can be funny. We may have to look for the funny a bit harder, or we determine that particular event is just never going to be funny. And that's okay too.

If Murphy's law is going to be twisted into anything that can go wrong can be funny, let's work together on how to practice finding the funny faster. Practice makes perfect, right? Remember that I'm a perfectionist.

If we look at moments in our lives where things have not gone as expected or anywhere close to expected, there is surely absurdity somewhere within it. That's what can make it memorable.

Some ridiculous incongruity, something that makes it so unique, that "stranger than fiction" moment which we can locate and find a way to laugh at, even if we cannot laugh at the event causing the trauma or loss.

That's also what makes us powerful in that moment.

I know I'm attempting to control a traumatic experience, a memory in my brain, but if I can control my trauma, or at least my reaction to my trauma, from triggering my brain to only remember the sadness or pain of the trauma every time, or even fewer times, it's worth it.

By controlling my past, I empower myself to control my present and even my future just a bit more.

CHAPTER TWENTY

Be Chipper

Sometimes the funny happens in the moment. When it's easy to find, it's an obvious joke, shared look between people, knowing glances, an eyebrow raised.

Sometimes the funny comes later, when people reminisce and process their loss.

Other times, it's never going to be found - that core memory will stay traumatic and painful, and that's just how it's going to be.

In an act of self preservation, we never touch it - years and sometimes decades later, that memory is "too hot to handle."

But as Gains and Berk taught us, memories are stronger, and more pleasing, when they incorporate humor.

We do have to value whatever our brains deem as "core memory material."

Even if we aren't sure which core memory shelf this one event is categorized into, even if we do not know the reason it's on the shelf in the first place, if I find something redeeming that happened during that time, within that event, or since that time related to that event, I can help transform the trauma or loss with a touch of humor.

As I am prompted to remember that core memory, when it comes back up to the surface, I'm meeting it with a little less pain.

I cannot erase some things, but why can't we reduce some of the pain?

I would love to be able to wave a magic wand or give you some solution that will inevitably just erase all of that, but I can't. Really, it's not at all fair.

It's now invested in you - in who you are, even though it alone does not define you.

There are whole theories on whether our DNA or our environments have a larger influence on us.

I'd like to say I knew the answer conclusively, but I tend to think it's both.

You are who you are because of your chemical makeup, who you are born from.

You are also who you are because of what you've gone through.

Those are valid statements.

We can't change either one of those statements, we shouldn't change them, but we can transform it.

Can we look for the lessons, find the value in saying "if I'm going to have to have that memory anyway, is there something I can do to help it be as painful?"

It was a Monday morning in early August. School would be starting soon, and my eldest daughter, an incoming freshman in high school, was trying out marching band.

Marching band is a noble activity - so many hours not only dedicated to learning and mastering a musical instrument, adding new music, and then walking to perhaps a different beat than the music you are playing. A standing ovation to all those who do it - and let's add 10-hour practices in insane midwestern August heat.

It's a noble activity - and not one that just anyone can do.

As we started week two of camp, I suspected correctly that she was not one of those interested in participating in this noble activity wholeheartedly. She tried a few different times prior attempting to get out of going to camp.

After all, it's hard work, in the beating sun, and for long hours at a time. I get it.

But we had decided that she would give it the old "college" try and finish the two-week commitment that she started, and then we'd reevaluate.

She got into the car, quite hesitantly, and complained of a pain in her neck. Something not right, couldn't straighten it all the way. She didn't think she could go to band.

I gave her a choice.

Band practice or the Emergency Room, attempting to call her bluff.

I have tried this successfully in the past. She *knows* we don't waste the healthcare professionals' time and her parents' money.

She honestly said she couldn't even move her head, turn it to the left or the right, or even bend it to get into the car.

She was in her room prior to leaving for band camp, applying sunscreen everywhere, because....midwest sunshine in August...and instant pain.

She was in tears.

We maneuvered her into the car, drove to the emergency room, and checked in. I still was skeptical about what could have happened that quickly, that severely, that caused her so much pain.

The triage nurse took a look at her, took her vitals, and sent us to a room. She had xrays and adjustments.

When the doctor entered, he diagnosed her with a pulled muscle and offered to give her a shot for the pain.

She hates needles. HATES. Had to be held down by multiple nurses for every inoculation prior to the age of 5 HATES needles.

She gladly agreed.

This was serious.

She was in an immense amount of pain and even the threat of needle didn't persuade her to disappear.

Band camp was officially off the table for the day.

She received her shot - in the butt - and I took her home and tucked her into bed. I checked on her once more before allowing her to sleep peacefully for a bit, moving on to the rest of my schedule for the day.

I was meeting my stepdad for lunch in another town, 30 miles away from home, after his dentist appointment. Although he had moved two hours away recently, he had not switched dentists, so this was a great opportunity to have lunch with me after his semi-annual appointment.

We planned on a steakhouse, so I set the navigation system toward that location.

On the way, I received a phone call (hands free) from the camp counselor where my youngest was staying overnight for two nights.

He explained that they had set up a slip-and-slide for fun, and my youngest had slipped and hit her head.

As a high school football coach, he was well versed in all things concussion, so he had administered a concussion check and determined that she did not have a concussion. He confirmed that with a nurse who was also on site, and she also did an evaluation and came to the same conclusion.

They had also asked my daughter if she wanted to stay or leave, and she said she wanted to stay, so they were just calling to inform me.

Both my girls were hurt, albeit mildly, but there wasn't much I could do about it, and they were handling it on their own.

I continued to my lunch date, and as I pulled into the parking lot, I noticed him standing by his car. It was a beautiful day, so I wasn't surprised by that.

When I parked next to him and got out of the car, he told me why he was standing outside. He had gotten out to go inside and get a table and realized he had just locked his keys in the car.

I did have a spare key, at my home, 34 miles north, and I offered to go retrieve it.

It would be faster than his spare, which was 111 miles west.

As we had the same insurance company, though, he asked if I would get my insurance card out of the car so he could use the number on the back of my card to call his agent.

We went inside and ordered our drinks and reviewed the menu as he called around to get an insurance agent and/or locksmith on the road to help.

As we were waiting for a return call from the insurance company and locksmith, we ordered our meals as I shared about my morning at the emergency room and my daughter's concussion status.

When the phone rang, it was for me.

My husband was calling - our 15-year-old first furbaby was nearing the end. It was time for him to go to the vet to become pain free.

This was not an unexpected call overall, but today, it was not part of the plan.

I sat stunned, having to make a choice. And also knowing, I couldn't really comfort any of my family in pain.

I couldn't get the key quickly and easily. I couldn't fix my daughter's neck, or my other daughter's head. I couldn't heal Chipper, the bestest dog on the whole planet.

I was very stuck in that I couldn't save anything, and it was frustrating.

But what I also saw, almost immediately, that OF COURSE every single person in my immediate wake would have a crisis at the same time.

What are the odds that would have happened?

That's the incongruity. That's the absurdity. That's the ridiculousness of our lives.

I will never forget the day we helped Chipper cross the rainbow bridge, as it's called.

Not just because of Chipper, but because of everything else that happened that day.

The neck healed, the head healed, the car was unlocked, the meal was delicious, and the dog's pain is less now.

None of it was in my control, but I found the absurdity, the silliness in the juxtapositions of all of it in one single August day.

I'm not ignoring the parts of sadness on that day, but I'm also not ignoring the absurd things. It's all part of the memory, and, therefore, the sorrow is cushioned in a little bit of something else, a little cloud of softness and silliness.

And who doesn't want or need a cloud of silly?

Chipper was named aptly because when we rescued him as a puppy, he was released from his kennel and pranced around all the other cages full of animals we had not selected, no noise, just happy, gleeful prancing. He was Chipper. I know he's even more Chipper on the other side of the rainbow bridge.

* * *

What is funny to you may not be funny to me, and that's okay.

Recognizing and anticipating humor are learned skills.

Author and educator Mary Kay Morrison describes the five stages of humor in her book Using Humor to Maximize Living.

She says that the first stage of learning humor is playing peek-a-boo.

When she first explained it to me as a form of humor, I was mortified as I realized what makes the game funny to us and also to an infant is that we are shocking the infant's brain in a way.

Essentially, we are comforting the infant by having a caregiver, someone who loves and cares for the baby, smiling in the child's face, and then we put up a barrier to that caregiver. We "remove" the caregiver.

This causes fear, albeit shortlived, in the infant so that when the barrier is removed and the caregiver returns, the baby senses relief and laughs, surprised relief which results in laughter.

It's the same feeling when we laugh after being scared or finding something startling.

It just seems a bit more masochistic when we think of it like this.

We all then fall into a category of baby torturer. Well, not really, but you'll never look at peek-a-boo the same way, I guarantee.

It's also how the brain reacts to stimuli.

The mirror neurons of the brain want to match whatever it sees.

If someone smiles at you, your brain instantly wants to smile back. Same for the opposing signals or reactions. If someone approaches you in anger, it takes a conscious effort to not respond immediately in anger as well. The brain wants to match, even if my 3rd grade shoes didn't.

The peek-a-boo stage lasts until around the age of 2, according to Morrison, but helps to build the trust that not only will the caregiver return, when they do, it will give a relief.

After all, humor itself is really just disruption in an expected pattern.

So when we think the parent is just always going to be there, and then they are not, and then they are again, that relief is what causes the laughter.

It's the early training on what humor and laughter can be in our lives, as well as how it can benefit our lives.

The second stage of humor which lasts from the age of two until the school age years is called Knock-Knock by Morrison.

While knock-knock jokes themselves are considered an advanced skill because of the steps involved, the expected pattern that emerges and the accessibility that "anyone can say them" or repeat them without much original humor skill makes them a perfect match for early humor education.

We should all remember when a child you know, or were yourself, attempted a knock-knock joke that was an original draft.

Sometimes they work, but often they don't - they are just plain gibberish.

171

The adults in our lives may laugh anyway, but the child is working through the incongruities and pattern of this humor stage, as well as learning that words can have more than one meaning or a combination of words that do not normally work together can be funny.

Students of humor are trying out a variety of punchlines and attempts, having learned that the jokes work for others, and are feeling their way through what works and what doesn't.

While we are encouraging the attempts at humor by laughing, the bigger laughs come when the jokes actually work, and the children of humor realize the difference pretty quickly.

The next phase of humor is called Riddle-De-Dee and shows up during the primary years, Morrison explains.

This stage of verbal irony is when jokes, riddles, and even sometimes clowns appear as humorous. Young students of humor practice jokes and repeat riddles, even trying to play with vocabulary and mixing words together that aren't normally funny or found together to create new or combined words.

The riddles often start, "what do you get if you mix a ___ with a ____?"

The joke can not only be found in the punchline, but also in the setup of the joke.

Remember elephino? If not, google it.

Morrison calls the fourth stage of humor Pun Fun, which is found in later primary grades as students enter and live in the middle school or junior high grades.

Here there is an increased understanding of words, language, and vocabulary. While a word may normally be used as a noun, trying it out as a verb has the ability to cause humor and laughter in audiences.

Plays on words are definitely not uncommon in humor, but it requires a grasp of the language by the joke teller and the audience.

As humor is shared by those who consider themselves to be included, or on the "inside" of the joke, the definitions need to be shared, which is why this is a later stage of humor.

For example, the food pun of "you're one in a melon" works if you know the audience knows you are trying to say "you're one in a million" but perhaps show a picture or are holding up a watermelon, cantaloupe or honeydew melon while you say the phrase.

Some puns result in laughter while some result in groans from the audience. Either way, it's a win, because the joke teller received a reaction.

Additionally in this stage, children of humor experiment with bodily functions and physical or slapstick humor.

These types of humor may have big rewards in laughter for the performers, but can also come at the expense of another person.

Humor isn't always a positive experience for joke teller and joke topic, so this is when hurt feelings and the standard retort of "it was just a joke" come in as a way to explain the use of humor.

More on the negatives later.

The double meanings of words is an elevated use of humor as it requires the elevated knowledge for all to get the joke. This is used many times in children's programming that is also enjoyable for adults. Adults will get different jokes or find situations funny that children enjoy differently.

Just because it's in animated form does not mean it's made for children, but movies that are animated with the targeted audience being children are also being made with a level of humor that is appealing to adults as the filmmakers know *someone* is bringing those children to the theatre or watching the movie on repeat at home and need their own source of entertainment within the same experience.

The adult-level puns and plays on words may go over the heads of the children or a double entendre joke related to sexual activity is ignored until a rewatch decades later gives the show new meaning for the child that once loved it more innocently.

When the humor reaches its full maturation, high school and up, Morrison calls it Joy-Flow because the "humergy," energy derived from humor - and Morrison's word - is passionate and optimistic.

This stage is when the humor child is finalizing their personal sense of humor, finding what types of humor are most energizing and relatable.

We do not all have to share the same sense of humor or find the same things funny.

Ideally, we are finding humor in positive spaces and manners, but there are ways for humor to be used incorrectly or as a weapon - which is a way that I do not recommend.

Positive humor creates an euphoric feeling and helps to reduce cortisol, the hormone that affects stress, in our bodies.

Humor is relief.

This joy-flow stage can be a combination of the previous stages and include wit, potty humor, physical comedy and more - whatever you find to be your sense of humor and what you honor in others.

As we learn more about what we like in humor, we recognize a similar style of humor in others and find attraction to them, in friendship or more.

One of the first skills we learn as babies is the ability to laugh, and it's one of the last things we lose at the end of life.

Other than breathing, there probably isn't a more important skill to hone than humor.

* * *

After you discover your sense of humor, you find that it magnetizes you to others who share the same sense.

This can be great, except if you're me and really want to be the center of attention.

I didn't want or need another class clown in the room, thank you very much.

So I became a teacher - captive audience, daily stage.

And they paid me?

Deal.

You may not find the same situation; however, there are benefits to producing humor and just being around humor, so even if you're not the class clown, you can still win.

Here's how.

First you need to recognize the numerous benefits of humor - and because I'm the president of the international Association for Applied and Therapeutic Humor, I'll share them with you.

Morrison also mentions specific ones in her book:

- Contributes to healthy mind/body balance
- Maximizes brain power
- Enhances creativity
- Facilitates communication
- Creates optimal learning environment
- Supports the change process

There are many more specific benefits of humor, because, as you may have heard, laughter is the best medicine.

That was something I just always believed, like knowing that humor was my superpower, what I used to cope during difficult or trying times.

I used it as a teacher to influence what I wanted students to do, how I negotiated my contracts, and how I made friends.

It wasn't until 2017 when I really immersed myself in the study of humor that I discovered all the research around it.

So while I may be a humor newbie in terms of the research, I've been a humor applicator for all of my life.

The research shows that laughter burns calories. Not a lot. But if you need to say, "I'm going to the movies" instead of "I'm going to the gym" to feel better about providing your body with exercise, go for it.

According to research conducted at the Vanderbilt University Medical Center, 10-15 minutes of laughter can burn approximately 10-40 calories per day.

Need more calories gone?

Laugh with friends.

Laughing out loud, which we rarely do when we are alone, increases both the heart rate and calorie expenditure by up to 20 percent, according to research published in the International Journal of Obesity.

The longer you laugh, the greater the effects, too.

Laughing out loud directly involves a minimum of 15 muscles, like "internal jogging," according to Dr. William Fry, an associate professor of psychiatry at Stanford University.

Dr. Earl Henslin, a doctor of clinical psychology, has studied humor and the brain for decades.

In his book "This Is Your Brain on Joy: How the New Science of Happiness Can Help You Feel Good and Be Happy" breaks down the specific impact humor has on reducing stress in all the parts of the brain, complete with brain scans of those who were in distress and then how that distressed brain looks when laughter is applied to it.

He concludes that the "long-term absence of joy" affects the brain negatively, but is not impossible to reverse.

So while we may have times where we find it impossible to feel or inaccessible to find joy, happiness, and laughter, once we do again, we can reverse any brain glitches.

Definitely encouraging news.

But how?

* * *

Humor researcher Dr. Peter McGraw in his talk titled "What Makes Things Funny" at TEDxBoulder explained how people of all ages and cultures experience humor on a daily basis and that humor itself even influences our choices, from what to watch to the people we date.

To prove his point, he told audience members that he was going to have them tickle their immediate neighbor in a few minutes after he explained his theory.

His Benign Violation Theory was created in his Humor Research Lab to explore how violations of moral norms make us laugh in situations using verbal and nonverbal communication.

For example, there is no violation of a norm when someone walks down the stairs. No violation, no funny. When someone falls down the stairs and is unhurt, there is a benign violation which can be funny. If someone gets hurt, there is a malign violation, not funny.

To eliminate the funny, we have to eliminate the violation. To make something funny, we have to add a benign violation - or remove the thing that makes it okay.

He says this is why tickling yourself doesn't work - there is no violation or threat of violation.

It also doesn't work because it's really difficult to sneak up on oneself and create that surprise that a lot of humor requires.

Dr. Paul McGhee published his first research on humor over 50 years ago, and has studied its impact and effects as well as habits that can be created to boost your creativity and use of humor in the workplace and in your life ever since.

In his book Humor the Lighter Path to Resilience and Health, McGhee discusses the need for humor in daily life, whether personally or professionally or both, and how humor or its absence can impact physical health as well.

We know that stress can impact physical well-being, or not so well-being, and humor can relieve that stress.

Determining which type of humor works best for you can be even on a case-by-case basis as you navigate your trauma, loss, and experiences.

CHAPTER TWENTY ONE

Put the 'Fun' In Funeral

When my baby sister Julie was born, I was already 5, fully engaged in being the big sister to Kristi, 3 ½ years my junior.

As Julie grew, I discovered we were very much alike - she was outgoing and adventurous, liking to explore around the house or even outside the house.

Our sister Kristi preferred to stay home with mom. We also liked mom, but we knew there were more opportunities to see something new *outside* the house than in it, so we were willing to travel a bit more.

Like 30 miles north to my grandmother's house overnight, for example. That's really traveling to a 7-year-old.

I now see how humorous it is that one of my daughters seems more like Kristi and the other more like Julie. As the oldest, I already feel like I helped raise them, and now I've been gifted the chance to do it again, so to speak.

Julie and I have always had a bond, which is different from my relationship to Kristi and her relationship to Kristi. The three of us together usually resulted in two against one - when you can break a tie, we did - and there were always hard feelings.

Growing up isn't easy.

But what we all shared was a bit of dark humor.

We got that from our mom. Remember her motto - we don't have a lot of money but we laugh a lot.

* * *

Mark Dinning released a recording of a song written by his sister Jean called "Teen Angel" in 1959.

The song is a lyrical journey through two dating teenagers whose car stalls on a railroad track. While they initially escape and are safe from harm, the girl runs back to the car as it is hit by the train, and she succumbs to her injuries.

When first responders pull her away from the wreckage, they find her boyfriend's high school ring in her hand.

The chorus of the song repeats "Teen Angel/Can you hear me? Teen Angel/Can you see me? Are you somewhere up above? And am I still your one true love?"

It is haunting, tragic, and surprisingly catchy.

My mother loved all sorts of music but found her "groove" in 1950-1960s rock and roll.

When the song was first released in October 1959, some radio stations banned it because of its tragic nature, deeming it too sad to play on the air.

Despite that, it reached the top spot of the Billboard chart in less than five months.

It was a favorite of my mom, probably of Mark Dinning's as well, as it was his only #1 hit.

He recorded music for another decade but cracked into the top 50 again of the Billboard's top 100 songs.

There is no thing in that story that is humorous - it's all tragic, indeed.

And yet, my mother dealt with the absolute morbidity of that song by not only sharing it with us, but also to create choreography that we could perform together every time it came on the oldies radio station she loved.

That is dark humor.

It's when something that is almost too much to handle finds humor as an outlet to process. It's also obviously an "inside joke," not meant for public audiences, because dark humor follows a different set of rules - more on that later.

* * *

Julie and I are also known for putting the fun in funeral.

We grew up attending Roman Catholic masses, with the traditional genuflection, standing, sitting, and kneeling at the appropriate times.

After enough visits, you know what to say, when to say it, and when to move, to participate in the ceremony.

When you're young, it can also be predictably boring.

That's true with anything that you don't get or understand the value of, no offense intended to any practicing Catholics at all.

We would find humor in most anything, and it would be sincerely difficult to hold back chortles, especially when we were supposed to be acting reverent and silent.

I might have found something funny when I was by myself, but I also knew I could control it better when I was by myself.

My sister and I have similar senses of humor so when I know something is funny to me, it is going to be dangerously funny to us both.

When the funeral directors approached us in the pews of the Catholic church, during the Catholic mass funeral honoring our sister's life, and asked us if we thought it would be a good idea to order more chicken as the church was standing-room only for the funeral mass, we laughed. During the ceremony. Because we remembered that during the time we only wanted to get a piece of chicken as we did our laundry while hosting the ICU waiting room in that St. Louis hospital, but the KFC was out of chicken.

The irony. The incongruity. The absurdity.

And, of course, we ordered more chicken.

And then very few came from funeral to burial to meal, so we froze the leftovers and had chicken for months.

I mean, we did get our chicken after all. Just a very long time later, and for a very long time after.

Julie and I have traveled great distances together and play off each other when we do, sometimes annoying, sometimes entertaining others.

Even in an emergency room.

* * *

Sadly, my grandfather on my stepdad's side passed away a few months into the beginning stages of the COVID pandemic. While he did not die because he contracted COVID, we strongly believe the isolation he had to endure at the veteran's home, for his own safety, in turn resulted in his rapid decline in health and ultimate turn for the worst.

He passed away in August, three days prior to his 92nd birthday, and his funeral and burial were slated for the following Saturday.

Due to COVID safety protocols in place, not many funerals were being held indoors, masks required, so we would do an outdoor ceremony. Typically in central Illinois, the muggy weather in August could be excruciating. Luckily, this day turned out to be sunny, warm, but not dreadful.

After a brief family-only, masked-up in-person indoor ceremony at the funeral home, we followed the procession to the cemetery, cars #5 and #6 in line.

Julie had mentioned that she wasn't feeling well, with some gastrointestinal symptoms, not respiratory as we knew to be more likely COVID at that time. I checked on her a few times, but she was determined to power through.

All of the attendees gave social distance during the burial, and it was being live streamed for anyone who couldn't be personally present or felt uncomfortable attending during the global pandemic.

Julie and her daughters stood approximately 10 feet away from me and my daughters, and easily 10 feet away from the immediate family - my stepdad, his sister and her husband, his brother and his wife.

As the ceremony neared the conclusion, I noticed out of the corner of my eye that my sister was increasingly in pain, as she clutched the middle of her chest and went with her daughters to her vehicle to rest.

I asked my daughters to stay put and went to check on her. Her daughters' faces were stark white with concern, as was Julie's - hers in pain.

Julie's eldest daughter could drive, so I instructed her to get behind the wheel and follow me to the emergency room.

In most cemeteries that I have visited, the driveable paths are quite narrow, allowing only one car's length at a time.

This was no exception, and I knew I now had to request the drivers of cars #1-4 to move their vehicles immediately after their father's ceremony to clear a path for cars #5 and #6 to head north to the ER.

I hated walking up to ask, but it was an emergency.

They, of course, quickly and quietly moved their cars and then we, in cars #5 and #6, proceeded to the Emergency Room.

Due to protocols and limits in visiting guests, I told my girls to stay in the vehicles and I would take Julie in and get her settled and then check back.

Still in an enormous amount of pain in her midsection, I motioned to the nurse at the entrance, and he brought out a wheelchair right away. We stopped at the sliding double doors to have temperatures taken, put on proper surgerical masks, and then were directed inside to the triage desk.

As we waited to be checked in, Julie's pain started to subside a bit, and her humor ramped up.

We joked, laughed, and bounced ideas and punchlines off one another, as we had for decades.

We were called up to the triage desk within five or so minutes, and the nurse proceeded to get all the vital information.

We were traveling to the funeral, nearly a four-hour drive from home for her. The hospital has to start with documentation from scratch. As they did so, we entertained ourselves with humor.

"What brings you here today?" the nurse asked, not knowing she was setting up a humorous story, and probably meaning what the reason for coming to the ER versus the reason to visit their town.

"Our grandfather's funeral," I responded.

Julie, without missing a millisecond, added, "Yeah, it was a little 'all about him,' so I had to make a scene," sarcastically.

It took the nurse just a few seconds to process my answer, which was an incongruity to what she had asked, and then the dark humor Julie was attempting about our grandfather's funeral.

Of course, we meant no disrespect to Grandpa, nor anyone grieving him, just trying to raise the humor quotient and release some of the pain at the same time.

She caught on quickly that we were joking, that Julie did not feel that grandpa was stealing her attention.

We continued to banter back and forth, sometimes including the nurse, and she laughed, and said, "Follow me."

Surprised that I was allowed back behind the doors in these COVID times, I excitedly pushed her wheelchair to a room and entered an examination room and then helped Julie into a hospital bed.

Over the next ten minutes or so, Julie and I greeted the staff who entered the room as long lost relatives, repeating their names, asking them questions about their jobs and procedures they were there to complete, and asking them how they were doing personally amid the pandemic.

We entertained ourselves and whomever was within earshot with humor, and released some pain along the way.

A nurse started an IV, and a doctor quickly was in to order some initial tests.

I soon realized that we would be here for a while, so with Julie's permission, I stepped out to the parking lot to inform the daughters of the status.

I told the girls she would be there for a while but she was feeling a bit better already, sending them to grab lunch a few blocks away.

I went back into the emergency room and asked the desk clerk how to get back to my sister's room.

She looked stunned and asked me to repeat my question.

"Yeah, I was just back there with my sister and came out to tell my daughters something and now I was going to go back in. How do I get there?"

"You were back here?" she stammered.

"Yes, just a few minutes ago."

"Really?"

"Yes, I just left to come out and tell my daughters something and just came back in."

Slowly, as if she didn't believe me, she cautiously said, "Okay. Just wait over there. I'll go check."

About ten minutes later, the original nurse came back out and came over to me.

"I'm so sorry. We're not supposed to let anyone back there at all," she explained, sheepishly, "and I was just laughing and enjoying you two that I completely forgot. You're only supposed to wait in this waiting area."

"Oh my goodness," I laughed, "no problem at all. I thought maybe you had changed protocol, but don't worry, I won't get you in any more trouble."

I asked her to take the things I had retrieved from my sister's vehicle to bring to her directly then, and went outside to join our daughters and wait for news.

The dark humor, the healing and release of pain, distracted even the nurse from her protocols. In this case, it was thankfully a harmless misstep.

But dark humor does have its dangers too.

* * *

Dark humor is sometimes called gallows humor, which is essentially grim and ironic humor in a desperate or hopeless situation.

It's when someone makes fun in a life-threatening, disastrous, or terrifying situation.

Is it helpful?

Is it healthy?

That may be up to the individuals to answer, but there are rules to using dark humor effectively.

The audience is crucial, and the mindset of that audience is critical.

Even if you have participated in gallows or dark humor with the exact audience before, it's imperative to "take the temperature" again to make sure the audience is in the same mindset or mindspace as the humor requires.

Because my sister and I grew up together, we are usually in the same audience and mindset, but not always.

I often know what she's thinking, where her mind may be going with a comment or thought, but not every time. It would be unfair of me to assume.

I still have to check in with her, or anyone else with whom I may have shared a moment of dark humor, to ensure she or they are in the same mindspace as I am at the time.

As with any humor, there is a risk, and especially with dark humor, it can be minimized by checking your audience and their mindspace.

Dark humor is not for public consumption – it's just simply not. It is a shared experience between people who are experiencing the same trauma or loss, at the same time, in the same way.

We know enough to know that not everyone could see the "fun" in the funeral. Julie even tried to put the "er" in funeral too. If only the nurse was named Al, we would have had the whole word.

The same trauma or loss, at the same time, in the same way.

That's a rarity – often found in pretty serious careers or situations where the levity is used not to make fun *of* the situation or any victim or circumstance, but rather to make fun *with the gravity of*, the severity of, the situation, trauma or loss.

Dark humor is frequently shared between first responders, military, healthcare, funeral directors, those who witness gruesome sights and situations who are using humor as a way to not feel shaken by those sights or to avoid taking those images home with them when the job is done. Gallows humor here is simply a way to vocalize the emotions without owning them as the trauma is not theirs – meaning their loved one isn't the one who needs or needed help.

Julie really didn't think the funeral was supposed to be about her – but making the joke about a heavy topic made everyone relax a bit. That surprise of humor is what is also allowing an opening for relief, allowing the brain to release the "feel good" neurotransmitters and endorphins.

In the middle of a long, horrific court battle for the permission to treat my mother humanely as her guardian, our dog was diagnosed with cancer.

We were told it was treatable, albeit expensive, and the tumor could be removed, so I scheduled an appointment to take her to the vet for her surgery.

It was a Friday afternoon, scheduled then due to their availability, not mine, but it certainly didn't hurt me to leave early on a Friday.

It was a beautiful day outside, sun shining.

I grabbed my things and made my way down the hallway to the exit when a colleague of mine, wonderfully kind, always-in-a-hurry-so-no- time-for-small-chitchat guy saw me heading out for the day.

His state of mind was amused.

Mine was not - it was preoccupied.

I had an ongoing court case that was draining - emotionally, financially, and literally my personal time bank from work - and I was not necessarily in a chitchatty or jovial mood for discussion of anything, let alone some sing songy interaction.

He said, "Off early on a gorgeous day?" There was no judgment, only celebration in his voice.

"Hope it's a great reason," he added, positively, with a sing-song in his voice and his heart.

"Oh, yep." I responded, matter-of-fact.

To match his sing-song in my voice, but not my heart, I added, "My dog has cancer."

His face fell. I kept walking.

This is an example of dark humor where the audience and mindset were not prepared, or involved.

I think about this interaction often, because I enjoyed some sick sense of relief from it, and worried, as I saw his face dumbstruck.

I never turned back, but I chuckled to myself, and then have suffered guilt since then, now years ago.

He wasn't in the same audience or mindset for that humor, and it was unfair to assume he was. Dark humor is a power that should be wielded with care as it can impact others more and differently than its intent. And I am responsible for both its intent and its impact to a certain degree.

Even if I use appropriate humor that is mistaken as inappropriate humor, I am responsible partially for the result, which means I often use low risk humor - where I poke fun at myself and my own mistakes.

Sometimes I use all my mistake stories in one single book. But don't fret, there are plenty more mistakes where these come from. And if I run out, I'll just make more.

CHAPTER TWENTY TWO

Find the Light in the Darkness

In 1975, The Mary Tyler Moore Show tackled the idea of dark humor on a much larger scale, as Chuckles the Clown from their own WJM-TV station was killed in a bizarre parade accident in the episode from season 6, episode 7, titled "Chuckles Bites the Dust."

The coworkers of Chuckles are trying to cope with their grief the next day as they process what happened and most of them cannot avoid making jokes, while Mary is appalled at their disrespect for their colleague as well as for how he died. The coworkers defend their actions, saying they are just kidding and finding relief from this disaster.

"Everybody does it," they argue.

She replies, "I don't," matter-of-factly.

At the funeral, the coworkers continue to joke until the start of the funeral ceremony, and then they become serene, respectful, and quiet. Mary, on the other hand, now cannot contain her giggles and chortles during the funeral.

This time, it is her colleagues, and the other people at the funeral, who are appalled at her behavior, but when the minister asks her to continue to laugh because that's what Chuckles would have wanted, she can no longer contain emotion - but it's not laughter that comes to the surface. It's sobs.

After the funeral, the colleagues discuss the reason behind their use of dark humor - as a means to process their fear of death.

The writer, David Lloyd, won the Emmy Award for outstanding writing in a comedy series for this episode, which routinely ranks in the top 100 television episodes of all time lists.

The colleagues at WJM-TV were in the same audience, but not always in the same mindspace.

When examples of dark humor are videoed and shared with an audience other than the one who had the shared experience, the results are much different than intended.

Intention is very important for the use of dark humor as well.

In Mary's colleagues' cases, they were intentionally using dark humor to release their stress, their fears, their worries. Mary's reactions at the funeral were unintentional.

Both are responsible for the intentions and impact that humor encountered, and sometimes that can be the tricky part.

* * *

As a high school teacher, I was blessed to be able to work with so many wonderfully talented, strangely quirky, and awesome teenagers over the decades of my career.

Some needed an adult to confide in, some needed a coach, some needed a little levity and lightness on a tough day, some needed an English teacher, some wanted nothing to do with me.

I was pleased with all of them.

Since starting my career in 1996, I guesstimate I have had over 1900 students in my English classes, if not more, and worked on theatrical productions, clubs or organizations that I sponsored, or fundraisers with easily another 600 students I never taught in my classroom.

Not only is that an enormous responsibility, it is also a great pleasure and power.

My intention for my English classroom was one of inclusion and comfort, light and levity.

A former student explained to a colleague this way about my sense of humor in the classroom, "if you understood her humor, you got her and enjoyed her class. If you didn't, you wondered how others could."

I know I'm not everyone's favorite - can't be - and even if our human nature is to always be liked, it's virtually impossible for it to be a reality.

I have connected with so many, and still so many keep in touch with me, for which I am so grateful.

I had one particular group of students who, after their graduation from high school, would make a point during breaks from their college lives to invite me to lunch while they were home from school to catch up. With me.

I was honored to be included in their lunches and loved hearing their progress, their stories, and honestly just watching their interaction with each other. Theirs was a beautiful friendship that spanned distance and time - not always something that happens with high school friendships, I have noticed.

During the spring break in 2013, we had yet to schedule our lunch as this break didn't exactly line up with the others' spring breaks.

I received a private message early one morning, telling me that one of those students had been killed in a car accident at the age of 19.

I am still stunned and shaken about this news.

We had been through quite a journey together. His sarcasm and wit matched mine, and he would often stay after school to decorate my classroom with jokes after I had headed to a rehearsal so I would arrive the next morning, raise the blinds, and see hidden pictures.

Many times I would cross paths with his family and converse about him. They were always so grateful for the time we had spent together.

During one of our "break lunches," I had shared my experiences about forgiveness with him, about my letter to my father, as he was struggling with similar circumstances. I encouraged him to write the letter, even if he didn't send it. *It could help*, I had said.

He was also very interested in his own appearance, meticulous details were important, and fashion as well. He often told me things I chose to wear were "atrocious." I declined to take his criticism to heart, because he said them in jest, even if he believed they were.

Devastated, I went to the visitation, which was held in the same church we had memorialized my sister at the age of 23 over a decade prior.

Again, the sanctuary was standing room only - and the line for the visitation to get near the family was a long wait.

It was somber and quiet, reverent.

To be in the church while a church service was not going on seemed strange - I hadn't done that often, even if my church was across the street from my parochial grade school.

As we approached the family, I searched my brain for something to say - something that would be meaningful, knowing full well that I had been on the receiving end of so many phrases that I would never remember and that nothing could really be meaningful.

I noticed his mom, her poise, her strength, and her gorgeous outfit. I then glanced at him in the nearby casket, dressed as he would have loved, looking handsome and "on fleek," as we had no doubt used incorrectly over the years.

I told her I was sorry for her loss, as we all probably have, looked her up and down, and then I added, "And he would have approved of your outfits."

She laughed.

A large, booming, church-shaking laugh.

I felt, and possibly heard, those present in the church gasp.

A laugh? At church? At a visitation?

She then hugged me tight, and we laughed and sobbed together.

No, it's not natural to bury your 19-year-old son. It's not. And nothing will ever make it right, or even understandable.

It makes no sense.

I didn't say those words for the intention of making her laugh. Honest. It was not my stage to perform. I said what I said to acknowledge that I knew her son, that I knew how much his appearance, and hers, for that matter, meant to him, and how I knew it was something that must have challenged her brain in the last few days.

I saw her. I saw her pain, but I also saw how she comforted his spirit and legacy and her own.

The laugh was a relief of being seen, of having "done something right" in a dark time.

She may not remember it, but based on the glares I received as I left the front of the church and returned to a pew in the back, much of the congregation assembled never forgot.

I felt peace at having provided a moment of levity for her.

I felt embarrassed that the others in the room didn't seem to get it.

As I returned to my seat, I gathered my things quickly and turned to leave when her sister approached me, hugged me, and said, "thank you so much for making her laugh. She needed it more than anything else right now."

We are responsible for both intention and impact.

Humor
Cushions

CHAPTER TWENTY THREE

Humor Restores

After teaching and working in a high school for almost two decades, a year shy to be accurate, I knew I was trying to juggle too many things - my court case, my mother's guardianship, a full-time job, motherhood, wifehood, extra bonus jobs, doctoral work, and a new part-time endeavor that was ripe to take off.

I asked my husband if we could afford me resigning as a teacher. Not only if we could financially swing my not being there anymore, but if he thought I could give it up.

He said, "I thought you should have left 7 years ago."

He knew that at some point I would "have enough" and want to leave, but it wasn't his decision to make. To be honest, I wouldn't have listened to him anyway. I would have also given him a hard time for trying to tell me what to do.

Ah, marriage.

But, he gave me the time and space to figure out what was right. At that time, under those circumstances, leaving was the absolute best move I had to make.

The other things in my life were non-negotiables. I could have quit them too or instead of, but I wasn't going to do that.

My platter was full, and I needed to quit something.

I paused my doctoral work - to someday finish the dissertation.

I quit teaching full-time.

I felt power, peace, when I submitted my resignation.

Within a few hours, though, I felt, as my neighbor-friend who had just months earlier done a similar journey said, "vomit-y."

I was not certain everything would work out how I had planned.

In fact, I was 100% positive it would not work out how I had planned.

I felt less "vomit-y" knowing I was doing the right thing for me, my mental health, and my family, knowing I had the support of my husband - financially, emotionally, knowing I had a superpower tucked in my back pocket - humor.

I knew something, anything, a lot of things, were going to go wrong, but I also knew a big chunk of them could be funny, and that's the mindset I needed to get me through the next year.

* * *

What do you get when you direct a musical with a 15-year-old who then goes on to become a lawyer in the exact field of lawyer you're hunting for exactly 20 years later?

You get a very comfortable relationship between client and attorney, and a lot of humor.

My need for an attorney was to support my mother and fight for guardianship of her after a stroke debilitated her.

She requested I take care of her needs, but as she had married someone new 10 months earlier, he was the official power of attorney by legal standards.

I employed this former theatre student of mine, and he worked tirelessly to meet my requests, answer my questions, and entertain my assumptions about the law.

"After all, I have seen every episode of 'Law & Order,'" I remember telling him.

"Oh," he replied, deadpan, "then you know everything."

"Exactly."

I laughed. Of course, I didn't, but this was no time to tell the truth - I wasn't under oath yet.

During the preparation for the trial, I badgered him with questions as any anxious person would, although mine might be a bit different.

"So, tell the truth, how many times have you had to stand up in court and scream, 'Objection! Badgering the witness!'?"

"Exactly zero times."

I was deflated.

"Really? Never? What a bummer."

"Yep," he said, "it's not like it is on TV."

We prepared again for court, and when the day arrived, I was extremely prepared, because I knew every square inch of this case - I had been obsessively running over the details in my mind for weeks. Another anxiety trick - to never let you think of anything else.

Because you may have not watched as many legal dramas as I have, I'll explain how this trial went.

I was the plaintiff, the one asking for something to be done, so my side went first.

A witness was brought in, sworn under oath to tell the truth, then my attorney would ask questions, called "direct examination."

Then the other attorney, for the opposition or defense, would ask questions, called "cross examination."

If the witness were deemed "hostile," as in the person may not be viewed as fair or just to both sides or "unfavorable," the cross examination question formation could be a bit more argumentative, starting with "Isn't it true..." which may look like badgering or torturing the witness, but in many cases, it is intended to bring about the truth because it puts the witness on the defense.

Then my attorney would get a chance to clarify answers with "redirect."

If at any time the opposing counsel was asking the question and the other attorney thought the question was inappropriate or breaking a legal procedure, the attorney on the opposite side says, "Objection" and then gives a reason.

You may have heard some of these - the common ones are "hearsay," as in the information provided has no proof and is just in conversation with; "speculative," meaning the question asks the witness to assume something but without evidence to support it; "irrelevant," the topic or question doesn't match the topic of the case; "leading," the attorney's question is helping the witness by suggesting answers; or "badgering," during a cross examination when the opposing counsel becomes hostile or asks argumentative questions.

Then the witness is released, and, in many cases, the witness is welcome to stay to watch the rest of the proceedings, if they so choose.

Because this was my case, I was in the courtroom from the beginning and watched every word, behavior, manner of question, ruling, and breath taken in that courtroom.

It was most of what consumed my waking and sleeping moments.

I was compelled to win, but not for me, for my mother - to give her peace, to help her when she couldn't help herself, and because she had asked me to.

I also have been around teenagers as an educator for decades and would notice patterns of behavior in students, enough to pretty accurately be able to predict their question, their need, or their ask before they had a chance to ask it.

The opposing counsel had a manner of slowly asking questions, methodically taking his time to craft a question, in the middle of it, and would take a minute or more to answer a full question.

This flustered many of my witnesses, most of whom I had not met prior to the requirement of this trial because they were not personal friends, but medical practitioners who gave unbiased testimony about what they had witnessed while providing my mother with medical care after the stroke.

While I tried to give them calm, reassuring glances from my table, they were often matching the opposing counsel's tone - which sounded calm but was condescending and hostile. When he asked a rambling, lengthy question, they responded with curt, short tones and argumentative responses.

Their responses were completely understandable, which was his intention, but it did not help my case to have argumentative, emotional witnesses.

My witnesses did not stay long on the stand, and they all provided much required evidence to help support my mother's wishes, but, emotionally, it was difficult on all of them.

All of my witnesses were brought in first, and my testimony was scheduled to begin on an early morning so I would have the entire time, if need be, to testify.

I was sworn under oath to tell the truth, and then entered the witness stand.

I was ready.

My attorney asked questions to set up my testimony for around 40 minutes. And then the cross examination began.

After the opposing counsel requested to treat me as a "hostile witness," I knew the line of questioning or at least the type of questioning to come, something my witnesses prior did not anticipate.

With every "Isn't it true..." question, I responded calmly, "No," and then explained what was true.

I referenced evidence both sides had produced at the trial already.

This behavior infuriated the counsel - he had yet to have a witness on my side who was as prepared, who knew how to anticipate his questions, and how to handle them.

His face grew redder, and I sat up straight and eager from the witness box, anticipating and prepared for the next attack.

He would have me on the stand for another hour, answering his lengthy and rambling questions expertly, if I do say so myself, and I do.

He became flustered at my quick and calm responses, and as he prepared the next question, I knew what evidence he was searching for on his table full of folders and cases of notes and documents.

He wouldn't be able to find the evidence, because it was a document that my side had entered, so it wasn't listed as an exhibit on his side.

As he hunted through his stacks, he asked questions of me, expecting me to take a while to answer or become overwhelmed and need at least a second to prepare, but instead, I answered quickly, calmly, and accurately each and every time.

Finally, he asked one more "isn't it true..." and as I shook my head, he got angry and approached the bench, repeating, "isn't it true...," the exact same question multiple times.

My attorney then rose and said, "Objection! Badgering the witness."

And I laughed briefly...inside, of course.

Decorum was of the essense.

The judge "Sustained" the motion, meaning the opposing counsel had to stop.

The opposing attorney then asked the judge for a brief recess so he could "find something," which the judge granted, and I was released from the stand.

As I approached the table, the opposing attorney came over toward my attorney. I located the piece of evidence I knew he was hunting for, put my finger on it, and slid it toward my attorney and said, "This is what he's looking for."

I then exited the courtroom as they both looked stunned.

During the break, I relayed the story to my sister who was not allowed inside the courtroom because opposing counsel "may need to ask her another question," so she could not be tainted by any other testimonies.

I said to my attorney as he approached, "Welp, can't say you haven't had to say those words now."

He responded, "Of course it would be with you."

We laughed at my 'Law & Order' moment. Even if I did have to have it without the iconic "dun-dun" music. I didn't want to pay for the royalties anyway.

This moment was not funny for the opposing counsel, and the whole trial was many more moments of tribulation than many of joy, but for these few hours, my expertise and the truth were winning.

We looked often for these glimpses of humor - and they didn't come as frequently as we would have liked - but when they did, they provided such relief, an opportunity to regroup, restart, and release some of the stress.

After the break, I returned for another hour on the stand, but the questions were a bit more subdued from the opposing counsel. Still rambling, though, don't worry.

The necessary evil of that trial was rewarded weeks later when the decision went my way, and I was awarded permanent guardianship of my mother, so she could have peace during her final days.

Law and order were restored, with a splash of laughter tossed in.

CHAPTER TWENTY FOUR

Humor Blends

"When you go through loss, trauma, your emotions are all put in a blender, with the lid off, turned on at full speed. You never know which emotion is going to come out next, at what velocity, and which direction it's going to go, but you know something is coming out that you may not be able to control," said Ryan Murphy, funeral director in central Illinois.

Those emotions can get everywhere, and the cleanup, while inevitable, may take a long while and may not be easy.

Murphy has been in the funeral business for almost a decade.

In that time, he has counseled numerous of families on how they want to see their loved ones cared for and even people preparing for their own demise and wanting to figure out all the details to help their loved ones avoid having to make all the plans, all the decisions, all the payments.

I had asked him during my mother's consultations and planning how he coped with a job that required him to be around sadness and sorrow and tears all the time.

An eternal optimist, he responded that he actually experiences a lot more humor than people expect.

Families come in to see him in the initial stages of bereavement and grief and, in some cases, with familial relationships that are already broken.

His job, he said, is to calm that fear and shock and help steer people toward selecting the right things for their families.

"I need them to know they chose the right person or people to take care of their loved one," he said quietly. "They need to know I will take care of them, so much that they don't have to anymore.

That gives them relief, which creates space for them to find laughter."

Murphy isn't necessarily unique to the funeral business, but his path getting there may have been.

He was 10 when his grandfather passed away.

"I was visiting him in the hospital. He wasn't moving, hooked up to all these machines and wires, for weeks," he recalled. "And then my mother said, 'he's gone,' and I was really surprised because - no, he wasn't, he was right there. And to me, he wasn't any different. He was still not moving, hooked up to wires and machines. I didn't get that he wasn't breathing anymore - everything looked the same to me."

This moment piqued curiosity for Murphy and, even subconsciously, he wondered how to help families go through these moments, how to ensure they knew someone was taking care of their loved ones, to help them through their grief.

"When you experience grief," he said, "you have to go through it. That's the difficult part, because going through grief isn't linear. You are mixed up with your emotions - they are in a blender for a long time."

"Grief doesn't get smaller," he continued, "we grow around it. We build things around it."

That growth creates the space for the humor and laughter to be connected to the memories.

Loss isn't just about the death of a person - divorce, end of friendship, job changes, moves, security, comfort, innocence, love, destruction, age, disease, and the list goes on.

What is universal in all of those is that grief is a necessary part of the moving on, but humor can be as well.

Adjusting the mindset can be a natural change, as Murphy found with many clients and families as they bury their loved ones.

"The initial meeting - my job is to just make them feel comfortable, as much as possible, in a very uncomfortable setting.

This may be their first or only funeral they have had to plan, but it's not my first or only one, and I remind them of that so they can relax a bit, but it is also personal and special to them and for their loved one," he said.

As they move through, in, and out of the stages of grief, they relax and find space for laughter and humor, he noted.

People think if they move around the grief, avoid it, that maybe it will just go away, that's a big misconception. Some people even physically move away from the location of where the event occurred or where the people are that share that grief. They put off the processing of the feelings until all of the ceremony or checklist is over, the busyness of the aftermath, he continued.

"That's when the blender opens wide," he laughed.

Some families opt to not hold a visitation or a viewing, to host family and friends because they don't really want to deal with it.

They might say, "I don't want to stand up there. I don't want people coming up to me and then saying, I'm sorry," he said, but he also warns his clients, "It's going to happen. People are going to approach you at the grocery store or somewhere else. That's why families choose to have the viewing or visitation because they can have most of those interactions in the same space and time, instead of dealing with those moments for the next six months or so as people run into you in public."

While you can't micromanage your grief, you can attempt to control it, until that blender erupts again, he said. Those who micromanage tend to find more eruptions earlier because they keep trying to put a lid on the emotions rather than allowing them to flow. Both are scary, both are important for growth, but both can also have disastrous consequences for the griever and for all around them.

The early stages of the global pandemic prolonged the relief that comes with a visitation or public burial, the closure, for many families, Murphy said.

"Families didn't get to see each other as we had to tell them in essence, 'choose your favorite 10 family members to be present,' especially during the winter months. As the weather improved for outdoor gatherings, we could add more people, but we were doing that to keep grieving families safe," he said.

A lot of the humor comes when families are planning the reflection materials - the boards of pictures, the slideshows for the ceremony or for social media, the stories heard from others as they think about the loved one. The stories no one else knew come out, the gratitude for the impact that person had on everyone else.

We aren't as sad to lose the physical being of someone else as much as we are saddened that we will not continue to have the direct impact or connection with the person lost.

We are able to, through the processing of grief and time and distance, to replace the feelings and images our brains conjure when those memories are triggered.

Murphy recalled the time spent with his own grandfather, the times sitting on his lap, World Wrestling Federation (then WWF, now WWE) together.

Their favorite wrestler - The Undertaker.

Even Murphy was surprised at that memory, insisting that the images and confusion surrounding his grandfather's death launched him into this career, but perhaps it was a joint, subconscious effort by grandfather and grandson.

Our memories are powerful. If we are able to package them a bit more consciously, intentionally, we can transform them with a little bit of light in the dark.

Some losses simply cannot handle humor at the same time, or ever. Murphy said there is rarely any use of humor around the unexpected loss of a young child. The gravity of that situation begs for release, but perhaps not with humor in this case.

Murphy said his biggest joys are watching the families and friends of the loved ones he works with finding relief or at least some processing of their grief during their brief time together.

"Our job isn't exactly just helping someone through all the planning and details. If they are in a dark room, we are providing a light at the top," he said. They will need to figure their own way out, "but here are the options for things they can do."

His rewards come in the form of helping them through this grief, including by not saying "no" to clients.

"We really don't like to say that, but during the early stages of the pandemic, we had to, which was devastating to the families, and to us," he explained.

Loss isn't just the death of a person, we know, but there is the ceremony usually involved in that when someone does.

Imagine if we had a funeral or visitation for the major losses in our lives when they don't involve the death of a person.

You may have your own moments of mourning, in private, but very few have a public showing of grief, where you can see a transformation, hear the laughter and stories of others who share a level of loss. That shared grief helps us grow.

When we are in the dark alone, we think the dark is growing because we cannot see the light.

Perhaps it's time to throw grieving parties, where we have those visitations, funerals, burials for the other things we are losing as well.

Graduations can essentially be a party that celebrates the loss of one chapter of life and moves us on to the next, for example. If we think of a way to have a gathering, to mourn a loss, and look forward to the next, reasonably it could help us move toward finding something funny or joyful faster.

Laughter is contagious. Robert Provine, Ph.D., studied several thousand examples of laughter and published his results in a 2004 article in Current Directions in Psychological Science where he discovered that laughter was 30 times more frequent in social situations - when we are alone, we are less likely to laugh, but just listening to someone else laugh can be enough to start a person laughing.

Laughter can also be used as a response to someone else speaking, but we are 46 percent more likely to laugh then whomever we are talking to - so not just hearing funny but sharing an anecdote or adding humor to our own speech, even as we retell our woes to friends and family.

A ceremony of sorts could be a gathering where we can do that, to help us find the funny faster.

People help us, even for you introverts out there.

Being around others who understand us, who want to comfort us, who want to help take some of our grief and loss away even if they cannot, will help us through the darkest times.

As we process the grief and find the way out, we often find ourselves helping escort the people around us through the grief too - children or family members who may not understand why this change is happening too.

We have been processing how trauma and loss impacts us throughout this book, but many of us are also in some ways responsible for the impact of what others in our lives are feeling and experiencing around these changes as well.

That can add a level of responsibility and management that can prolong dealing with our own needs, as finding that balance of helping someone else manage and grieve changes and time for ourselves can be exhausting and seem nearly impossible.

It can be done.

You can do it.

And humor helps.

CHAPTER TWENTY FIVE

Humor Challenges

Can musical theatre help you grow grit? Does the phantom hide his face?

If you don't know the answers to both of these questions, we may need to get you some grit and/or theatre training, which I happily volunteer for both.

Dr. Ronald A. Berk, professor emeritus, bio-statistics and measurement, from The Johns Hopkins University, has been studying the idea of grit, started with Duckworth in print in 2007, for years, evaluating others' studies on grit and connecting it to academia and other areas of life.

He concluded in his 2018 paper "Grit 2.0: A Review with Strategies to Deal with Disappointment, Rejection, and Failure" that grit can be improved and elevated with a growth mindset or specific interventions to improve grittiness, some of which are musical theatre references sprinkled throughout all Berk does from papers to presentations (and I'm here for it!), but also with humor.

Duckworth herself mentions the four ingredients to organically grow grit - interests, practice, purpose, and hope.

Humor can be used to connect them all, but most of the time humor provides relief and hope.

And you can teach yourself to hope.

You can also teach yourself humor. How to humor, that is.

The biggest lesson you can learn about humor is that you don't have to BE funny to find humor. You can find the funny faster without ever telling a joke. You just need to find your brand of humor, things that bring you light and joy and make you chuckle, guffaw, laugh out loud.

How many times have you used the LOL acronym only to not honestly laugh out loud at whatever you just claimed to laugh out loud at?

My guess is since you're a human living in these times of texting, you have sent the "lol" text nearly 1.2 million times and actually laughed out loud only a small fraction of those times. In fact, I personally send "lol" to things I do not laugh out loud at but find myself laughing out loud at things I would never send a "lol" reply to.

Anyone else out there?

As we have covered before, there are so many different styles of humor - ranging from slapstick and physical comedy to word play to potty humor and a combination of them all.

If there were just one perfect way to get to humor, it would definitely be a lot easier to manage stress and find peace quicker, but we are all unique people that like different things and laugh at different forms of humor.

Sorrow and sadness is universal and, across the globe, a sad story is a sad story. It makes you have similar emotions no matter the language used to tell its story.

Humor is not the same. While humor is universal and its benefits are unparalleled, its construction, delivery, timing, and forms are all unique to the deliverer and its receiver.

Sometimes it even comes down to when you receive humor. The same story or joke may not resonate with you now, because perhaps you haven't experienced anything like what is being described, and then later, you revisit that same story or joke and now you "get it."

I felt that way with parenting humor before I was a parent.

I "got" some of the jokes and stories prior to being a parent, but after I became one, I "got" a lot more of the inside humor of those stories, because I was able to relate to them more then.

Some people think they have different senses of humor and they cannot change those, but, like grit, you develop more skill and personal growth in many areas as you age and experience more events - both in grief and joy.

You can enhance your humor, alter it to different circumstances or audiences, and simply just find things funny in a variety of ways.

Not all humor has to be in our faces, outlandish and slapstick. Humor can be subtle, understated, dry or sarcastic.

The beauty of it - you get to pick.

Like selecting your favorite music genre or movie style, you may have a preference for a particular type or style of humor, but even those crossover artists or moments surprise us.

Perhaps you're not a country music fan, but a country artist creates a mashup of country music and something you do like, and you find a gateway into liking another style of music.

Humor can work the same way.

Maybe you like humor that is a bit risque or maybe you don't like comedians or performers who work "blue," using sexual innuendo or profanity into their jokes or stories.

Normally.

But in a rare instance, when exposed to the artist or type of story in a different way, you may find yourself evolving and liking that style or just liking that particular moment in time.

No judgment either way, just asking you to keep an open mind to ways positive, affirming humor can enter your consciousness and become part of your memories.

* * *

Humor can be approachable.

Here are some ways to get your humor habit started:

Lin-Manuel Miranda was right - you should "smile more." You don't necessarily need to talk less, but smiling more does two things - it activates your brain to accept joy or happiness, and it tells others you're ready to give and receive the same. The mirror neurons in your brain are set in motion to take whatever it witnesses and try to match it.

Make the brains of others around you have to match your smile.

No more hiding, here are some direct challenges to help you find the funny faster.

Direct challenge #1 - Smile More.

Direct challenge #2 - Get Silly.

When we take ourselves too seriously, serious things get us down. I know, we know, there are times when we have to be serious, when things have to get done, but do they have to be done all the time so seriously.

Yes, in a court of law, but everywhere else? There have to be places to get silly. If you feel ridiculous when you're being silly, you're doing it right.

Direct challenge #3 - Find a Humor Buddy - or a Humor Hero. Someone you connect with, share a similar sense of humor with, or just admire their use of humor with others can keep you in a positive frame of mind - or to at least allow you to steal with positive energy for a little while when yours is low.

Direct challenge #4 - Watch Something Funny. Whether you are discovering a sitcom or movie for the first time or even participating in a strategic, whole run-of-show rewatch (I see you Office Ladies), viewing something funny puts us in an addictive mindset - one that craves more laughter, humor and joy.

If watching something you've seen before still brings you joy, do it. As many times as you'd like. Otherwise, there's not much explanation for 67 billion minutes of The Office being streamed in 2020.

Funny videos on whatever platform makes you happy also work for quick humor breaks. They help you relieve stress so you can get back to the seriousness you need to have sometimes. And brain breaks and humor breaks boost productivity.

Direct challenge #5 - Exaggerate. We all know that as the distance between our event and our retelling of the same event grows, our telling of them can grow in details or exaggerations. That's okay to play with the facts that aren't as important. Obviously, you don't want to perjure yourself or intentionally tell untruths but exaggerating the details can lead to humor or at least humorous aspects of the story which makes the recalling of it more bearable.

Reframing or retelling the same story from a different perspective also allows for humor. The retelling of the Wizard of Oz from the perspective of a wicked witch gave its audience a different and greater perspective in the musical Wicked, for just one example.

Whether you use humor personally or find humor, knowing how accessible it can be if you just look for it will guide you to find the funny faster as you approach your next disappointment, trauma or loss.

You deserve to be happy.

You deserve to have joy in your life.

You are the source of joy for someone else too.

Using humor to transform your memories of trauma or loss even just a small amount makes them more accessible.

And that's the permission you need to move forward.

Humor and grit work together to make you a resilient survivor.

* * *

Now that you have a few more humor hacks under your humor hat, let's review.

Here are some questions that you can use to help you as you move through the stages of G.R.I.T. to find the funny faster after a new loss.

THE G.R.I.T. WORKSHEET

Answer these 5 questions in each of the G.R.I.T. Method sections to help you move from grief to transformation of your loss with humor.

G - Grieve

1. Are you grieving honestly? Authentically? Are you hiding your grief to save face or spare others' feelings?
2. What feelings make you the most uncomfortable right now? Start with those first.
3. What does my life look like now without what I have lost?
4. Am I embracing the pain and feeling all the feelings or hiding them away from even me?
5. How am I doing with managing ADLs - activities of daily living? (showering, brushing my teeth, eating, sleeping, laundry, etc.)

R - Relate

1. Who can I reach out to to discuss my feelings over this loss?
2. Who knows what this feels like? Or something like this?
3. What gives me comfort right now?
4. What is my favorite memory from what I have lost?
5. What have I used before to help me get through other tough times?

I - Invest

1. What things in my life am I most enjoying right now?
2. Are there things I have given up on in my past that I need to rekindle? Should I try those hobbies again?
3. Are there others I know of who are hurting that I could help by reaching out to or checking on?
4. Is there anything I have always wanted to do but never did but could now?
5. What's one simple thing I can do right now to move myself in a new direction?

T - Transform

1. When was the last time I laughed about anything with a friend?
2. What is my favorite comfort comedy - a show, a person, an activity, an image?
3. In five years, when I look back at this loss, what do I hope to remember that brings me joy or makes me smile?
4. Am I living in this moment? Am I preparing for a future moment?
5. What is one memory of this loss that has humor around it?

These questions can be used to guide you as you transition through your event, relive a seemingly settled one, or process one yet to be faced.

CHAPTER TWENTY SIX

Humor Teaches

When I was in my sophomore year of college, first time living away from home, relying only on myself to do my laundry, I was thrilled that in my residence hall, just one floor below, we had access to coin laundry services.

The girls of my hall had determined a plan to leave a laminated card with the floor and room number of the person using the machine so that when the cycle was completed, if the machine was in need of someone else, they could contact the right clothing owner.

After a weekend where many of the students left campus, three floors of residents were called into an emergency meeting.

The residence hall leaders informed us all that over the weekend, someone had placed poop in the machines.

As this was the time period before security cameras were available, no one knew for sure who was responsible, but they knew the machines had to be serviced, if not replaced, and that someone had to pay for it.

The university was not going to be that someone.

As it had to be a resident, or a guest of a resident who had let the culprit into the building, they were going to split the cost with everyone in the three floors, whether they were present or not, unless the guilty party or parties came forward.

From an administrative standpoint, it makes sense to use peer pressure to draw out the guilty party. After 20 years of teaching teenagers, though, I have found that most will not come forward, especially if they would have to pay for the whole thing if discovered, but if not discovered just have to pay a small portion.

Not every teenager I have met would avoid accountability, but it's just a part of the decision making or rationale that's missing until around the age of 26 when the frontal cortex of the brain becomes fully developed.

To be honest, I don't remember if we ended up paying for it or not. I remember the reaction to the news of the incident in the first place, and I remember the complaining by all of us for being responsible for something we had no part in.

It's gross. I will never think otherwise. I will never think that was funny, even if it wasn't my clothing in the dryer.

What I do remember is wondering, how no matter how much that machine is cleaned, how the remnants of what happens will always be a part of it. Somewhere, hidden in the nooks and crevices that we don't think about often, some little bit of that evidence will remain.

Simply, I would have fundraised to replace the machines - and that is quite possibly what they did.

I often think about trauma and loss and how to cope with it using humor, and I am always reminded of the "crap dryer" story.

That trauma and loss will always stay with us, in the crevices of our memories, even when we think we have handled it completely, processed it fully, cleaned the mechanics of our brains, or even eliminated all traces of it.

We know it's still there. We can sense it, even as we go through our daily lives. It's there. It won't ever not be there.

Right alongside it, however, is hope.

The hope that not every day is going to be filled with an incident like this. Not every day will have a time where you have to pay for someone else's choices. Not every day will have remnants of the stuff people have left behind because they didn't deal with their own stuff.

Every day will have an opportunity for you to share about your experience, though, and to learn from it. Use it to teach ourselves. Use it to teach others.

What are your traumatic experiences, your feelings of loss teaching you?

At the beginning, they are teaching you how to get through hard, difficult, seemingly impossible times. There is no doubt.

As you continue to process and find the funny, you can look again at what that is teaching you or has taught you.

I often tell my girls a line I first heard attributed to noted clinical psychologist turned television talk show host Dr. Phil McGraw, although I cannot say he was the first or only one to have said it:

"You teach people how to treat you."

We are constantly in a process of training others about us - what we like, what we don't, what we accept, what we will not. People around us learn (or don't) by those interactions what our limits are and what we are willing to do or not do.

If I respect my boundaries, and say no, they may not ask again.

If I don't have the time to do another task but I say yes anyway, they will ask again because I have said yes before.

Both are fine reactions. These are just examples of what I mean because they both have a payoff - I'm getting something out of each interaction.

If I say no, I'm protecting myself - the payoff is me and my time, but I may want to be asked again and that risk may not pay off.

If I say yes even when I don't want to - the payoff is pleasing the other person, giving them what they want, which may not be a big risk for me, but it might depend on the situation.

You have to make those decisions, those choices.

In those, we teach the people we are around how to treat us.

In order to teach others about us, we need to know about ourselves. Remember, we need to be our own best friends.

We have to know our values, treat ourselves well, tell others what we need, set those boundaries, express gratitude for things we do like, and forgive ourselves and others when we and they get it wrong.

These things, unfortunately, do not protect us from trauma and loss, experiencing grief or pain, but they do help us prepare to move forward.

So what are your stories, your experiences, teaching you?

I'd love to know - shoot me an email and share a story you're willing to share with me - jenniferjkeith.com.

And then, tell others.

Share your stories, your heartaches, your heartbreaks, AND your lessons with others.

As a high school teacher, I was surrounded by drama, and not just from the teenagers - but that's for another book.

Teenagers that loved to cause conflict, those who loved to be around conflict, those who found energy from conflict, and those who avoided it like a global pandemic.

On one particular afternoon, a few students in my freshman level classes entered my classroom, gossiping about some little drama that they were not personally involved in but were sharing it as if it was happening to them in real time.

I stopped them and quickly shared the "crap dryer" story.

Of course, they found parts humorous, and some parts unfair. Some parts were humorous, and some parts were unfair.

The lesson is here (and no, I probably didn't sound as eloquent as I'm trying to here, but the lesson is the same):

"No matter what you do after you step into that dryer, you are not getting rid of that crap. It's on you, it's around you. You can clean yourself a hundred times, but the fact will remain, you may still smell, or at least thing you do.

When you enter into a situation that isn't where you belong, it's nearly impossible to remove yourself from that situation without impacting it or it impacting you.

Maybe you can change the situation. At what cost? Will it impact you more? Will it do you more harm than good?

Sometimes you may need to be involved to save the others from being harmed. Sometimes you may think you need to be involved but the people in there have chosen to be in there and must find their way out on their own.

But you have to ask yourself this:

Do you want to roll around in that forever?"

The lessons aren't always clear. I didn't think at the time we had our residence hall "who threw the poop in the dryer" meeting, *oh, I'll use this in teaching teenagers someday.*

You may have to really dig to find one or create one. And maybe there isn't one we ever see.

What we do know is that humor, healing, finding the lessons, all take time, effort, and practice to be successful.

You should do it.

You can do it.

You will laugh again.

You have grit.

You have resilience.

You are worth it.

Humor heals.

Humor helps.

ABOUT THE AUTHOR

Forget flying, invisibility or teleportation - the best superpower to covet is humor. Jennifer Keith's superpower has been and always will be humor - in many forms.

As a certified Humor Professional and current president of the international Association for Applied and Therapeutic Humor, Jennifer discovered the brain remembers two things - trauma and humor. Using her G.R.I.T. method of using humor to process trauma and loss, Jennifer finds ways to fix the funny bone and find the funny faster when surrounded by disappointing and upsetting events. If your brain is remembering the difficult times anyway, why not cushion them with a little bit of light, levity, and laughter?

Jennifer has degrees in English, journalism, theatre, technology, and educational leadership, proving that she doesn't want to nor should any of us grow up or stop learning. She encourages you to take funny bone breaks - integrating humor into daily life, career, and family situations which can transform situations from barely tolerable to memorably positive.

Jennifer recently added TEDx Speaker and author in the same month to her extensive resume of educating and laughing at the same time.

Jennifer lives in central Illinois with her husband, two daughters, and puppies.

Follow her at jenniferjkeith.com for all of her next steps.

ACKNOWLEDGEMENTS

Thank you:

To my husband Ryan Keith for enabling me to set the boundaries I needed to get the book and edits completed, and, most importantly, for sharing my life with me these last 19 years. We have created a remarkable family of human and fur babies and humor. Thank you for making me laugh.

To my first born, Gracelyn, for showing me that I don't have to be loud to lead, and that there's nothing like a great book to read and share with others. Thank you for allowing me to tell some stories of my failures as a parent, of which you had a front-row seat.

To Emersyn for inspiring me to get to the publishing arena by beating me to it as only 11 years old. You also teach and remind me how to love others all the time.

To my sister Julie for sharing our childhood each and every day. It wasn't easy all the time, but as your "fun in funeral" partner, I have learned more than most that it's so much easier to survive when you laugh – and you make me laugh more than most.

To Gay, John, Rick, Kay, Bob, Gayle - my parents who have shaped who I am and set the stage for who I'm still striving to be

To my therapist of over 6 years who will pretend to not be bored reading these stories again or will highlight the ones we haven't discussed so we can tackle those next. Thank you for "getting" me and for always giving me valuable homework that I can ace.

To all my besties I've met along the way, you know who you are, (if you think it's you, you're right) who listened endlessly about different story pitches and planning for this book and provided valuable insight and encouragement. I'm incredibly blessed by and grateful for each and every one of you.

To Jen Hatmaker and Glennon Doyle - thank you for sharing your truths on the page and on the stage. You have inspired me to laugh, love, feel, and share all the pains and joys without shame or fear. You both taught me to love, do the hard things, and carry on. Proud to be a warrior with you.

To Ashley Mansour and Jessica Reino of LA Writing Coach for the TAP Method, your notes and encouragement, and overall cheerleading of every author you work with. I was blessed by your feedback and coaching and know I wouldn't have completed it as quickly without you.

To my Author Accelerator class of Spring 2022 - Veronica Carey, Andy Way, Jessica Singh, Morgan McIntyre, Katelyn Davis, Samantha Kaaua, Juan Dias Rivera, JoAnna McSpadden, Leslie Bost, Linda Daugherty, and Vanessa Molina - you have inspired me in so many ways as an author and cheerleader. I know you're going to crush your author goals and it was my pleasure to write with all of you.

To my mentors and colleagues in humor: Karyn Buxman, Dr. Lee Berk, Dr. Gurinder Bains, Peter Derks, Mary Kay Morrison, Dr. Earl Henslin, Dr. Peter McGraw, Dr. Paul McGhee, Dr. Robert Provine, Dr. Ronald A. Berk, and countless others in AATH – thank you for your valuable contributions and research

To Ryan Murphy for sharing yourself and your career with me and so many people in central Illinois. You are comfort and warmth when others need it most.

To the Association for Applied and Therapeutic Humor and all my fellow Certified Humor Professionals, I'm immensely grateful for the study and fellowship over the last several years that provided me with the knowledge and confidence to publish this information for the world to see. This organization NEEDS to be known worldwide in droves - more now than ever before. We are serious about humor. Join us. www.aath.org

To all my former and current students, colleagues, friends, bosses, and more - I am so grateful our paths crossed and that you shared yourself with me. I'm the lucky one.

To anyone else who I neglected through no fault other than my own, I'm so terribly sorry to have overlooked your contribution. I'm also sorry for any typos found in this manuscript. No extra credit for finding errors!

To you, the readers, I hope this book is something to help you grieve, relate, invest and transform. May you find the funny faster and faster every time life gives you a surprise.

For a complete list of bibliographic information and anyone I omitted in this or that list, please go to www.jenniferjkeith.com

Printed in Great Britain
by Amazon